THE CATHOLIC UNIVERSITY OF AMERICA
CANON LAW STUDIES
Number 84

THE JURIDICAL FORM OF MARRIAGE

AN HISTORICAL CONSPECTUS AND COMMENTARY

A DISSERTATION

Submitted to the Faculty of Canon Law of the Catholic University of America in Partial Fulfillment of the Requirements for Degree of

DOCTORATE OF CANON LAW

BY

JOHN JOSEPH CARBERRY, S.T.D., PH.D., J.C.L.,
Priest of the Diocese of Brooklyn

THE CATHOLIC UNIVERSITY OF AMERICA
WASHINGTON, D. C.
1934

Nihil Obstat:

VALENTINUS T. SCHAAF, O.F.M., J.C.D.,
Censor Deputatus.

Washingtonii, D. C., die X Maii, 1934.

Imprimatur:

THOMAS EDMUNDUS MOLLOY, D.D.,
Episcopus Brooklyniensis.

Brooklynii, die XII Maii, 1934.

Printed by
THE PAULIST PRESS
New York, N. Y.

TO MY MOTHER AND FATHER

TABLE OF CONTENTS

PART II

LEGISLATION OF THE CODE CONCERNING THE FORM OF MARRIAGE

CHAPTER III

CHAPTER IV

CHAPTER V

CHAPTER VI

CHAPTER VII

CHAPTER VIII

FOREWORD

From the earliest days of her history the Church commanded the public celebration of marriage, and urged the parties to receive the sacerdotal blessing. However, in the light of the testimony of the early centuries and according to the unanimous opinion of writers, the assistance of the priest at Christian marriage was not a requisite for its validity. Marriages contracted without witnesses or solemnities of any kind were recognized as valid. They were severely forbidden and frequently penalties were attached to the laws which forbade them, but nevertheless their number increased. The root of the evils of these secret unions was the impossibility of establishing the exchange of true matrimonial consent by testimony other than that of the parties concerned. From this source flowed the greatest harm to family life and society at large.

In the course of time it was realized that a more drastic remedy was necessary if secret marriages were to be checked. The first general law of the Church against secret marriages was made at the Council of Trent, November 11, 1563, and expressed in the familiar decree *Tametsi*. According to the terms of this new law only those marriages would be considered valid which were contracted in the presence of the parish priest and two witnesses.

The decree *Tametsi* was the law of the Church for three centuries and more. It had been well planned, but was executed in a manner which proved an obstacle to its complete success. Certain modifications were found to be necessary, and these were embodied in the decree *Ne Temere* which was published by the Sacred Congregation of the Council, August 2, 1907. The decree *Ne Temere* was a studied endeavor to clarify and simplify the former legislation concerning the celebration of marriage. This decree ceded to a revised legislation of the form of marriage when the Code of Canon Law was published in 1918 for the Universal Church.

The present dissertation is a commentary on the legislation of the form of marriage as contained in the Code of Canon Law. It is not concerned with the liturgical form of marriage, or the religious ceremonies which surround the celebration of marriage. Its object is the juridical form of marriage as contained in the canons 1094-1099. A brief resume of the legislation which ante-dated the law of today is added in the hope that it will be of service in understanding the development of the present law. The historical summary is not an exhaustive study of the question, for the lack of sources and the length of time which such a work would require rendered it impossible. The historical notes which have been collected are given with the hope that from them a broader view of the question will be had.

The writer wishes to express his sincere appreciation and gratitude to the Faculty of the School of Canon Law for their kind and helpful direction,. to Rev. James T. Clancy, A.B., S.T.B., J.C.B., for his assistance in preparing the dissertation for the press, and to the many others who have aided and encouraged him in the preparation of this study.

PART I

HISTORICAL CONSPECTUS

PRELIMINARY DISCUSSION

THROUGHOUT the course of the history of the Church the term "clandestine marriage" has been used with more than one meaning. Sometimes it signified a marriage for which no evidence was available save the testimony of the parties; or a marriage contracted in the presence of witnesses, but not *in facie Ecclesiae*. After the IV Lateran Council (1215), a marriage was said to be clandestine, when the prescribed banns were not published. Later, after the Council of Trent, the term was applied to marriages contracted without the presence of a priest and witnesses, as had been decreed by that Council.[1]

Clandestine marriages had always been an evil. "Clandestine marriages, as they are productive of many evils in society, have always been discountenanced in well constituted governments; and have been always been deemed more detrimental to the peace and good order of a nation in proportion as it has been civilized." [2] The evil of such unions was that there is often no proof that there has been a marriage. Aside from the testimony of the parties there was no evidence that there had been an exchange of true matrimonial consent. Hence quarrels easily arose, fierce hatred developed, the parties separated, and sometimes remarriage followed. "It not infrequently happened that a man who had thus pledged himself, afterwards regretted the folly of which he had been guilty and proceeded to make bad worse by a new marriage publicly celebrated with all due solemnity. The difficulty was now inextricable. The true wife could obtain no redress. To have accepted her unsupported statement would have been to put all future marriages at the mercy of any unscrupulous woman who chose to perjure herself to the effect that the bridegroom was her husband. Even if the man repented his crime, his admission of a previous contract could not possibly be entertained. The whole story might be pure fiction devised as a means

[1] Wernz-Vidal, *Jus Canonicum*, V, 530, note 21; Joyce, *Christian Marriage*, p. 107, note 2; Gasparri, *De Matrimonio*, 3 ed., n. 49.

[2] Gally, H., *Considerations on Clandestine Marriage*, p. 2.

to escape the marriage-tie which had become hateful to him."[3] In such marriages hereditary rights were often endangered, a shadow could be cast upon the legitimacy of children, and innumerable occasions of sin were fostered. Conflicts between the internal and external forums might easily arise, as in the case of a man who had secretly married, deserted his wife, and then remarried publicly. If he wished to clear his conscience he would be obliged to leave the woman who was legally his wife, and his union with his true wife would be looked upon as concubinage.[4]

It is not necessary to dwell upon the evils of clandestine marriages. Yet from the viewpoint of the natural law clandestine marriages were admittedly valid since they contained the essential requirements for a valid contract such as marriage, namely, the consent of the parties who were competent to marry, and this consent reciprocally manifested in words, signs, or in any other way whatsoever.[5] On the other hand, however, marriage is something more than an agreement which concerns only the parties to it; marriage is the foundation of the family, it adds a new unit to the State. The relations, duties and obligations which flow from the marriage contract are of supreme importance therefore to the individual as well as to society in general. Hence it is that competent authority in society may step in and for the benefit of the common good restrict the right possessed by the natural law to contract marriages secretly, and super-impose conditions and solemnities which must be observed by all in order to contract a valid marriage.[6]

The conditions and solemnities which competent authority lays down for the valid entrance into the marriage contract constitutes the form of marriage. The competent authority in some cases may be the civil law; for baptized persons it is the ecclesiastical law. This

[3] Joyce, *Christian Marriage*, pp, 107, 108.

[4] Joyce, *Christian Marriage*, p. 109. For further discussions of the evils of clandestine marriage, *cf. Concilii Tridentini Diariorum, Actorum, Epistolarum, Tractatuum, Nova Collectio*, IX, 642, ss.

[5] Wernz-Vidal, *Ius Canonicum*, V, n. 523; De Smet, *Betrothment and Marriage*, I, n. 103.

[6] Benedict XIV, Const., *Paucis abhinc*, 19 March, 1758—*Fontes*, n. 447; Leo XIII, Ep. Encycl., *Arcanum*, 8 February, 1880—*Fontes*, n. 580

dissertation shall be concerned with the form of marriage as it is prescribed in ecclesiastical law. The ecclesiastical form of marriage therefore may be generically defined: "The solemnities which must be observed by virtue of ecclesiastical law in the contracting of marriage." [7]

The definition given expresses the meaning of form of marriage in its wide sense, denoting namely all the conditions and solemnities which are to be observed at a marriage in virtue of ecclesiastical law. Of these some refer to marriage as a contract while others concern it directly as a sacrament; the former is called the *juridical form,* the latter, the *liturgical form.* Since marriage is both a sacrament and a contract at the same time when both parties are baptized (canon 1012), it is seen that these distinctions constitute but different aspects of the same object. The *juridical form,* looking at the contractual aspect of marriage, consists of certain conditions which must be observed for the valid and lawful contracting of marriage. The *liturgical form* is comprised of the rites and ceremonies with which the juridical form is observed; it consists of ceremonies which are prescribed in the Ritual or permitted by laudable customs.[8] The present dissertation, however, plans to study only the juridical form of marriage which may be either substantial or accidental. The substantial juridical form consists of conditions which must be observed for the *valid* entrance into marriage; the accidental juridical form are the conditions which are required for the lawful celebration of marriage, not for its validity.[9]

In the decree *Tametsi* the Fathers of the Council of Trent left no doubt about their attitude towards clandestine marriage for they stated that the Church had always abhorred them and had prohibited them for very grave reasons.[10] The Fathers of the Council, however,

[7] Wernz, F., *Jus Decretalium,* IV, n. 209; Vlaming, *Praelectiones Juris Matrimonialis,* 3 ed., II, n. 553.

[8] C. I. C. Canon 1100; Rituale Rom., tit. VII, c. 2, *Ritus celebrandi matrimonii sacramentum,* n. 1-5.

[9] Payen, *De Matrimonio,* II, n. 1754; Vlaming, *Praelectiones Juris Matrimonalis,* II, n. 553; Wernz-Vidal, *Jus Canonicum,* V, n. 524, 526; Duschene, *Christian Worship,* p. 428.

[10] ". . . nihilominus Sancta Dei Ecclesia ex iustissimis causis illa semper detestata est atque prohibuit . . . "—Conc. Trident., sess. XXIV, *de ref.*

did not settle the question of the validity of clandestine marriages during the centuries which preceded the decree *Tametsi.* They merely stated that such marriages were without a doubt valid as long as the Church did not declare them invalid; but as to the *fact* of the Church ever passing legislation by which they would have been invalidated they remained silent.[11] It seems to be generally admitted, however, that historically clandestine marriages were considered valid prior to the Council of Trent and that the first universal law of the Church which established a substantial form of marriage was embodied in the decree *Tametsi.*[12]

The historical resume concerning the form of marriage which is to follow will be contained in two chapters, the first treating of the celebration of marriage in the Church prior to the Council of Trent; the second, dealing with the juridical form as established by the decree *Tametsi,* its subsequent development, and its modification in the decree *Ne Temere.*

matrimon., c. 1; *cf.* also Benedict XIV, *De Synodo Dioecesana,* lib. VIII, c. 12, n. 4, 5.

[11] "Tametsi dubitandum non est clandestina matrimonia, libero contrahentium consensu facta, rata et vera esse matrimonia, quamdiu Ecclesia irrita non fecit . . . "—Conc. Trident., sess XXIV, *de ref. matrimon.,* c. 1.

[12] Gasparri, *De Matrimonio,* 4 ed., n. 929; Wernz-Vidal, *Jus Canonicum,* V, 526, note 5; Vlaming, *Praelectiones Juris Matrimonialis,* II, 553; Leitner, *Lehrbuch des katholischen Eherechts,* p. 188; Freisen, *Geschichte des canonischen Eherechts,* p. 138.

CHAPTER I

THE CELEBRATION OF MARRIAGE PRIOR TO THE COUNCIL OF TRENT

ARTICLE I. ROMAN LAW AND THE FORM OF MARRIAGE

ROMAN law recognized two types of marriage (*iustae nuptiae*), marriage *cum manu*, and marriage *sine manu*. They were named from the juridical consequences of each marriage. In marriage *cum manu* the legal status of the wife was altered completely. She came under the power (*manus*) of her husband's family, and became subject to the *paterfamilias* of his family.[1] In marriage *sine manu* the wife retained her identity, remained unchanged in her legal status. This type of marriage was known as free marriage and predominated in the classical period of Roman law.[2]

According to Gaius marriage *cum manu* existed in three forms, namely, *usus*, *confarreatio*, and *coemptio*. *Usus* is described as a form of marriage by which a year's unbroken cohabitation of a man with a woman gave him *manus* over her, provided the purpose of the union was marriage.[3] *Confarreatio* consisted in this that the marriage was celebrated before the *pontifex maximus* and the *flamen dialis* in the presence of ten witnesses. It was called *confarreatio* because in the celebration of it the husband and wife were required to break and eat together a cake made of meal.[4] From the ceremonies it would seem that this form of marriage was reserved to the patrician class. The sources are silent about the obligatory value of the ten witnesses mentioned, and it is not known whether they were required

[1] Gaius, *Inst.*, I, 115 b; II, 86; III, 82; Greene, *Roman Law*, p. 47; Sherman, *Roman Law in the Modern World*, II, n. 470.

[2] "At the most splendid period of Roman greatness, the fashion of wedlock amounted to little more than a temporary deposit of the woman by her family" Sir. H. Maine—Greene, *Roman Law*, p. 49.

[3] Gaius, *Inst.*, I, 111.

[4] Gaius, *Inst.*, I, 112; *Regulae*, 9; Servius, *in Georg.*, I, 31.

for the validity of the marriage.[5] *Coemptio* was a form of marriage in which the bridegroom bought his bride by a fictitious sale.[6]

At the time of Gaius marriage was mainly a consensual affair. He regarded *coemptio* and *confarreatio* as additions for special purposes to the usual celebration. *Usus* was obsolete. The three forms of marriage which have been described were not substantial forms, that is, solemnities which had to be observed for the validity of the marriage; they were forms of establishing *manus* over the wife. If it could be satisfactorily established that one of these forms had been observed, there could be no question of the subjection of the wife to her husband.[7]

In the Rome of the classical jurists, *manus* was no longer a living institution, and Corbett observes that "it was a matter of legal archaeology." [8] Instead, in this classical period free marriage, or marriage *sine manu,* prevailed and to it was applied the rule set forth by the jurists of the Digests, *"Nuptias non concubitus sed consensus facit."* [9] The Romans clung tenaciously to the principle that consent was the constitutive element in marriage, either the consent of the parties if they were *sui juris,* or of their *patresfamilias* if they were *alieni juris*.[10] Roman law sealed the matrimonial union when the consent of the parties could be established, whether the proof rested upon the testimony of others, or upon facts. There were certain presumptions that matrimonial consent had been given such as *traditio rei domesticae,* or *traductio mulieris in domum mariti*.[11] It is generally agreed, however, that Roman law did not set up a juridical substantial form of marriage such as exists in canon law today.[12]

During the late Empire so much attention was paid to the dowry

[5] Corbett, *The Roman Law of Marriage,* p. 75.

[6] Gaius, *Inst.,* I, 113, 123.

[7] Corbett, *The Roman Law of Marriage,* pp. 68, 86.

[8] *Op. cit.,* p. 91.

[9] D. 50, 17, 30.

[10] D. 23, 2, 21; D. 23, 2, 2; C. 5, 4, 14.

[11] D. 23, 2, 5; C. 5, 3, 6.

[12] Freisen, *Geschichte des canonischen Eherechts,* p. 101; Meier, *Jus quod de Forma Matrimonii Ineundi Valet,* p. 16; Corbett, *Roman Law on Marriage,* p. 68; Wernz-Vidal, *Jus Canonicum,* V, 525; Joyce, *Christian Marriage,* pp. 41, 42; Sherman, *Roman Law in the Modern World,* II, n. 475.

and pre-nuptial gifts that the belief became prevalent in some quarters that they were necessary for the validity of the marriage. To offset this belief Theodosius II and Valentinian II in 428 A. D. issued a law to the effect that the omission of these formalities in no way affected the validity of the marriage.[13] Justinian embodied this law in his Code, and repeated it in one of his Novels.[14] Justinian, however, required the pre-nuptial arrangements for the validity of marriages between senators and ex-actresses.[15] From these laws it will be noticed that witnesses were required for the marriage celebration. The texts of the laws, however, do not reveal whether the presence of the witnesses was required for the validity of the marriage.[16]

Justinian limited somewhat the generality of the legal maxim *consensus facit nuptias,* when he forbade persons of high positions to marry without a previous dotal contract [17] and stated his reason for this legislation as follows: "For, as it has been set forth in ancient constitutions, and also established by Us, that marriages celebrated without dotal agreements and prompted by affection alone, are valid and durable, but as the country is already full of fraudulent contracts (for witnesses are constantly introduced who, incurring no risk, testify that a man called a woman with whom he was living his wife, and that she alluded to him as her husband, and by means of such statements marriages are presumed which in reality have never

[13] "Si donationum ante nuptias vel dotis instrumenta defuerunt, pompa etiam aliaque nuptiarum celebritas omittatur, nullus aestimet ob id deesse recte alias inito matrimonio firmitatem si inter pares honestate personas, nulla lege impediente, fiat consortium, quod ipsorum consensu atque amicorum fide firmatur" —*Cod. Theod.*, III, 7, 3.

[14] "Si donationum ante nuptias vel dotis instrumenta defuerint, pompa etiam aliaque nuptiarum celebritas omittatur, nullus aestimet ob id deesse recte alias inito matrimonio firmitatem, vel ex eo natis liberis jura posse legitimorum auferre, inter partes honestate personas, nulla lege impediente consortium, quod ipsorum consensu atque amicorum fide firmatur"—*Code,* V, 4, 22. *Cf.*, also Novel, XXII, "Nuptias itaque affectus alternus facit dotalium non egens augmento."

[15] *Code,* V, 4, 23, 1.

[16] Joyce, *Christian Marriage,* p. 188, note 3.

[17] "In majoribus itaque dignitatibus . . . neque fieri haec omnino patimur sed, sit omnino dos et antenuptialis donatio et alia omnia quae honestiora decet nomina"—Novel, LXXIV, 4.

taken place), it becomes Our duty to provide for these cases in accordance with the natural law." [18]

In the case of "persons who occupy places of less importance and discharge honorable duties, or are members of respectable professions, if they desire to marry lawfully without the ante-nuptial contract, they shall not do so indiscriminantly, without security, without proof," but must have their marriage attested by the official of a Church, and three eclesiastical witnesses, and registered in the archives. Justinian explains this: "We order, however, that this rule shall be observed when there is no dotal agreement or ante-nuptial agreement is made, for the reason that we consider the marriage which can be proved only by witnesses as suspicious." [19] The position of the ecclesiastic however in this regard would seem to have been no more than that of a civil registrar.[20] This registration was not required for every class. "Anyone who is of abject condition, is the owner of little or no property, and is hardly able to obtain the necessities of life, shall have permission to marry without making any contract." Likewise, soldiers in service, farmers, and this "in order that children born of such marriages be legitimate." [21] Later, in the year 542, Justinian published another Novel in which he said he wished to make the regulations more exact which he had already laid down in Novel LXXIV. In this new law the marriages of *illustres* (the aristocratic class), and higher dignitaries must be marked by the conclusion of the marriage contract if the marriage is to be valid.[22] In the same law he declared that the marriages of those outside this special class valid when contracted through mere affection. In this Novel, Justinian seems to have established a substantial form of marriage for the *illustres* and higher dignitaries; it was a

[18] Novel, LXXIV, 4—English translation, S. P. Scott, A.M., *The Civil Law,* Vols., XV-XVI, p. 283.

[19] Novel, LXXIV, 4; Joyce, *Christian Marriage,* p. 195.

[20] Meier, *Ius quod valet de Forma,* p. 16; Roberts, *Banns of Marriage,* p. xiv.

[21] Novel, LXXIV, 4.

[22] "Et propterea jubemus eos qui maximis dignitatibus decorati sunt usque ad illustres, non aliter nuptias celebrari nisi dotalia scribantur instrumenta"—Novel, CXVII, 4.

civil form of marriage, however, for the assistance of the cleric is not mentioned as in the previous Novel.[23]

Article II. The Celebration of Marriage in Canon Law

1. *Celebration of Marriage Among Early Christians*

It is certain that as early as the third century Christians ordinarily received the sacerdotal blessing at marriage,[24] and the custom very probably goes back to the Apostolic times. From the beginning Christian teaching stressed the sacredness of marriage for Christ had raised marriage to the dignity of a sacrament [25] and had declared it to be one and indissoluble,[26] and the Apostles preached this doctrine to the world.[27] It is only natural therefore to expect that the Christians should regard marriage as something sacred, and seek the blessing of their priests when entering into it.[28]

The earliest reference to the assistance of the priest at Christian marriage is perhaps that which is found in a letter of St. Ignatius to Polycarp, in which he says: "It is becoming that marriage should be contracted with the advice of the bishop, so that the marriage

[23] Meier, *Jus quod de Forma Matrimonii ineundi valet,* 17.

[24] "If the question be first concerning Christians marrying one with another, by whom the solemnity of the marriage was performed, by the minister of the Church or another, I answer, that it is most probable, that in fact for the first three hundred years, the solemnities of marriages were usually performed by the minister of the Church"—Bingham, Rev. J., *Christian Antiquities,* VII, 332; *cf.* also, Gothofredus, *Commentarium in Theodosian Code,* III, 7, *de nuptiis,* 31; Benedictus, XIV, *De Synodo Dioescesana,* lib., VIII, 12, 3; Joyce, *Christian Marriage,* p. 186.

[25] Conc. Trident., sess. VII, *de sacramentis in genere,* canon 1; sess. XXIV, *de matrimonio,* prooemium, canon 1.

[26] Conc. Trident., sess. XXIV, *de matrimonio,* canon 2; *de ref. matrim.,* c. 1, 7.

[27] 1 Peter, III, 7; St. Paul, Ephes., V, 32.

[28] "Christianity gave back to marriage its religious character. The founder of the Christian Church had not prescribed any ceremonies in connection with it, but in the earliest times, the Christians of their own accord asked for their pastor's benediction"—Westermark, E., *The History of Human Marriage,* p. 427.

may be according to the Lord, and not according to concupiscence." [29] Tertullian is more explicit in his reference to the priestly blessing. He stresses the fittingness and the happiness of a marriage which has been blessed by the priest. "Whence are we to find adequate words to tell fully of the happiness of that marriage which the Church conciliates and the oblation confirms, the benediction seals and the angels announce, the Father holds for ratified." [30] In another instance Tertullian reveals the attitude of his time towards secret marriages. "Among us secret marriages, that is such as are not publicly professed before the Church, are in danger of being considered as fornication and adultery." [31] Pope Siricius refers to the priestly blessing in these words; ". . . if the blessing which the priest gives to the woman who is about to enter on conjugal life be violated by a breach, the faithful regard her act as a sacrilege." [32] Pope Innocent I writes in a letter: "We are taught that the blessing which is conferred on the bridal pair by the priest . . . is an observance of a law instituted long since by God." [33] St. Ambrose has declared: "When marriage ought to be sanctified by the sacerdotal veil and benediction, how can that be called a marriage where there is no agreement on faith." [34]

The same insistance upon the priestly benediction of marriage, and publicity of the celebration is to be found in some early Councils. A canon in the ancient collection of decrees which is known as the *Statuta Ecclesiae Antiquae* has the following: "When the bridegroom and bride are to receive the priest's blessing, let them be conducted to the Church by their parents or by the paranymphi . . . " [35] In the Council of Arles marriage was forbidden to take place without a

[29] St. Ignatius, *Letter to Polycarp,* c. 5—M. P. G., V, 723.

[30] Tertullian, *ad Uxorem.*, II, c. 9—M. P. L., I, 1302.

[31] Tertullian, *De Pudicitia,* c. 4—M. P. L., II, 987.

[32] *Ep., ad Himerium,* c. 4—M. P. L., XIII, 1136.

[33] Ep., 2, *ad Victricium,* c. 6—M. P. L., XX, 475.

[34] St. Ambrose, *Letter to Virgilius,* c. 7—M. P. L., XVI, 336.

[35] "Sponsus et sponsa, cum benedicendi sunt a sacerdote, a parentibus vel a paranymphis offerantur in Ecclesia sacerdoti"—Mansi, III, 952. Hefele (*History of the Church Councils,* II, 410), gives the date of the council as 398, but notes that it is not certain that the council issued these laws, and he believes that the statutes are of later origin than the Council of Carthage to which they are usually attributed.

public celebration.[36] The Council of Verno, 755, prescribed that every marriage be public whether the parties belonged to the nobility or not.[37] Several Pontiffs repeat the same idea. Pope Hormisdas urged the public celebration of marriage and the reception of the priestly blessing when he decreed: "Let no one of the faithful, no matter what his standing in society be, enter secretly into marriage; but with the blessing of the priest let him marry publicly in the Lord." [38] Pope Nicholas I (858-867) in his reply to Prince Boris of Bulgaria described the practice current in Rome for the celebration of marriage. After mentioning that the marriage should be arranged, and the consent of the parents obtained, he continues: "And first of all they [the parties] are led to the church of our Lord, bearing the offering they make to God by the hands of the priest, and thus they receive finally the blessing and the heavenly veil." [39]

After the German peoples were converted to Christianity, they continud to adhere to the practices and ceremonies which had been handed down to them from their ancestors. In most of these peoples marriages was normally accompanied by the transfer of authoritative guardianship (*mundium*) over the bride from her parents or natural guardian to the husband; he was thus constituted her *mundoaldus.*[40] The transfer of *mundium* required the observance of certain prescribed formalities both at the betrothal and the actual marriage. At them the bride was given to her husband and then ceremoniously conducted to her new home and installed as its matron and mistress. Only a marriage thus contracted was called a *matrimonium legitimum,*[41] and it took place publicly in the presence of friends and relatives of the parties. A prominent part was taken

[36] "Nullum sine dote fiat dos, nec sine publicis nuptiis quisquam vel uxorem ducere praesumat"—c. 6, C. XXX, q. 5.

[37] "Ut omnes homines laici publicam nuptiam faciant tam nobiles quam ignobiles"—Council of Verno, canon 15—Mansi, XII, 583.

[38] "Nullus fidelis cuiuscumque conditionis sit, occulte nuptias faciat sed benedictione accepta a sacerdote publice nubat in Domino"—c. 2, C. XXX, q. 5.

[39] *Decreta Papae Nicolai I*—Mansi, XV, 402.

[40] Huebner, *History of Germanic Private Law,* Vol. IV, Continental Legal Series, p. 597; Meier, *Jus quod de Forma Matrimonii Ineundi Valet,* p. 9; Joyce, *Christian Marriage,* p. 48.

[41] Joyce, *Christian Marriage,* p. 48.

by a person styled among the Germans as the "Fürsprecher." It was his office to inquire of the bridegroom whether he had come for the purpose of marrying the woman; and then to put the same question to the bride and her guardian. This manner of celebrating marriage remained in Germany for many years.[42] To these ceremonies of the German people following their conversion were added the sacred rites of Christianity, and especially the priestly blessing.[43] Because of the length of the ceremonies, and their nature (some could not be fittingly accomplished in the Church) they were enacted *"in facie Ecclesiae,"* on the outside of the Church, and afterwards the parties entered the Church to attend Mass and receive Holy Communion.[44] The blessing of the priest was looked upon with the greatest reverence, and it was considered of such importance that it was prescribed in one of the Capitularies of Charlemagne.[45]

2. *Juridical Value of Presence of Priest at Marriage*

It is readily evident from the testimony which has been thus far presented that (a) Christian marriages were blessed by their priests and (b) that secret marriages were forbidden. It is natural to ask whether the priestly blessing and publicity of the marriage were so essential to the marriage celebration that the marriage would be invalid without them. In other words were they required as a substantial form of marriage. At the Council of Trent, as has already been mentioned, some Fathers were of the opinion that the priestly blessing had always been required as an essential condition for the validity of marriage. Whether or not this was true ought to appear from the testimony of the Fathers, Pontiffs, and early Councils which testimony has just been given. An examination of this evidence

[42] Friedberg, *Das Recht des Eheschliessung,* p. 25; Von Hormann, *Tridentinische Trauungform,* p. 17.

[43] C. 17, C. XXVIII, q. 1, *cf.* also *Dictum Gratiani;* Huebner, *History of Germanic Private Law,* IV, 603.

[44] Huebner, *History of Germanic Private Law,* IV, 605.

[45] "No marriage should be celebrated any other way but by blessing with sacerdotal prayers, and oblations and whatever marriages were performed otherwise should not be accounted true marriages but adultery, concubinage or fornication"—Mansi, XVII, 1062.

seems to indicate very clearly that the public celebration of the marriage, and the blessing of the priest were not conditions affecting its validity, but were only requisites for its lawful celebration.

The references of St. Ignatius, Tertullian, St. Ambrose, the various Pontiffs, and the canons of the several Councils mentioned may be interpretated to contain an obligation of precept only, and not an essential condition for the valid contracting of the marriage. The Christians were urged to receive the priestly benediction in order that their marriage might obtain more graces and fuller blessings.[46] The capitulary of Charlemagne was a civil law, and was enacted primarily in order that marriage within prohibited degrees of kindred might be prevented.[47] Pope Nicholas I clearly manifested the prevalent opinion with regards to the validity of marriages which were not blessed by a priest. Certain Greek priests had assured the Bulgarians that no marriage was valid unless it had received the sacerdotal blessing.[48] They asked the Pope's opinion concerning this statement. In his answer the Pope described the formalities which were customary in the Roman Church in regard to weddings (among which he referred to the nuptial blessing), but he expressly declared that these solemnities are not essential to the validity of the marriage.

> We do not say that any sin is involved, if not all of this is observed in a marriage, as the Greeks, you tell us, would have you believe: especially since it often happens that some are hampered by such extreme poverty that no help is forthcoming to enable them to prepare such celebrations:

[46] Benedict XIV, *De Synodo Dioecesana*, lib. VIII, c. 12, 5.

[47] "Ut incestis nuptiis et seipsos et ceteros maculare non praesumant antequam episcopi presbyteri cum senioribus populi consanguinitatem conjungentium diligenter exquirant: et tunc cum benedictionem jungantur." *Capitulare Aquisgranense* (802 A. D.)—M. G. H., *Leges*, I, 95.

[48] *Cf.* Constitution of Leo the Philosopher (886-911) in which he prescribed the blessing of the priest as an essential condition of validity. "Matrimonia confirmarentur sacrae benedictionis testimonio, adeo ut, si qui citra hanc matrimonium ineant, id ne ab initio quidem ita dici, neque illos in vitae illa consuetudine matrimonii jure potiri velimus"—Novel LXXXIX. With regard to this civil law, Benedict XIV has the following: "Verum haec Constitutio, cum a Principe laico prodierit, non potuit matrimonii validitatem quoad conscientiae infringere"—*De Synodo Dioecesana*, lib. VIII, c. 12, n. 6.

> and on this account let the simple consent of those whose wedding is in question be sufficient, as the laws prescribe. If this consent be lacking in a marriage, all other celebrations, even should the union be consummated, are rendered void.[49]

Buchard of Worms (1025), instructed the confessor to inquire of his penitent if he has contracted marriage without the offices of the Church, and without the proper formalities. In the event that he had done so, a penance is assigned to him, but nothing is said about leaving his consort.[50] Clandestine marriage, therefore, while a grave breach of ecclesiastical law, is nevertheless a valid marriage.

Gratian bears testimony to the validity of marriage contracted secretly and without the priestly blessing: "Marriages which are contracted secretly, are not denied to be marriages, nor is a dissolution of the union ordered, if they can be established by the confession of both parties. But they are forbidden, for should one of the parties repent of the step, the judge cannot accept the confession of the other as evidence."[51] In another place, Gratian distinguishes between a marriage at which the civil and religious ceremonies are duly observed, and a marriage where these are disregarded, and the partners are content to take each other as man and wife by mere consent. The former he terms *matrimonia legitima et rata,* the latter simply *matrimonia rata,* that is, sacramental marriage which is valid in the sight of God.[52] Pope Alexander III leaves no doubt as to the validity of a marriage which has been contracted without the presence of the priest:

> In regard to the matter which your letter has brought to my notice, *viz.*, that a certain man and woman, by command of their lord, exchanged a mutual consent, no priest being present, and without the ceremonies which the English Church is wont to observe, and that before the union was consummated another man married the aforesaid woman with the customary solemnities and knew her; we have

[49] *Decreta Papae Nicolai I,* Mansi, XV, 402; c. 2, XXVIII, q. 2.

[50] *Libri Decret,* XIX, c. 5—M. P. L., CXL., p. 958.

[51] C. 9, C. XXX, q. 5.

[52] *Dictum ad* c. 17, C. XXVIII, q. 1.

> judged that the following answer should be made by your prudence: If the first man and the woman received each other by mutual consent *de praesenti* saying respectively . . . even though the customary solemnities did not take place, and the union was not consummated, the woman must be restored to the first man since after such consent she could not, and ought not to marry another.[53]

The teachings of distinguished theologians support the validity of marriages contracted without the priestly blessing. Peter Lombard is clear in this regard: "In the celebration of this sacrament, as in the others, there are certain things which belong to the substance of the sacrament: such as the *consensus de praesenti,* which of itself suffices for the formation of the marriage; and there are also things which belong to the dignity and solemnity of the sacrament, as the giving of the bride by her parents, and the priestly blessing . . . "[54] The teaching of St. Thomas is to the same effect: "The words by which the matrimonial consent is expressed are the form of this sacrament, not the priestly benediction, which is a sacramental."[55]

In the debate during the Council of Trent on this question reference was made to a decree of Pope Evarist according to which the priestly blessing seemed necessary for the validity of a marriage. The letter is found in the Pseudo-Isidorian decree, and cited in the principal collections of canons.[56] The passage from the letter of Pope Evarist which refers to clandestine marriage is as follows:

> A *matrimonium legitimum* cannot otherwise be formed than if the woman is asked in marriage from those who appear to have authority over her . . . and if at the proper time, the priestly blessing is conferred upon her (as is customary) in connection with the prayers and oblations by the priest. . . . Have no hesitation in reckoning unions formed in any other way not as marriages but as adulteries and simple

[53] Compilatio I, c. 6, *de duorum sponsatione,* IV, 4. *Cf.* also Compilatio II, c. 1, 2, *de clandestina desponsatione,* IV, 4.

[54] Petrus Lombardus, *IV Sent.,* D. XXVIII—M. P. L., CXCII, p. 934.

[55] St. Thomas, *IV Sent.,* lib. IV, D. XXVI, q. 2, Art. 1, ad 1.

[56] Hinschius, *Decreta Pseudo-Isidorii,* p. 87; c. 1, C. XXX, q. 5; for discussion in the Council, *cf.* Benedict XIV, *De Synodo Dioecesana,* lib. VIII, c. 12, n. 5; Pallavicinus, *Hist. Conc. Trident.,* XXII, c. 4.

cohabitation . . . unless the purpose of the parties concerned has supplied the deficiency and lawful marriage vows have rescued them.

According to this passage it would seem that marriages which were not blessed by the priest were to be considered adulteries. An examination of this letter, however, will show that it has not much force in proving that the priestly blessing was required for the validity of marriage. In the first place, according to Berardi, this letter could not have been written by Pope Evarist, for it does not agree with the times in which he lived. Hence it cannot be considered as authentic.[57] As a revelation of the times in which the letter was written it is of value to show that the absence of the priestly blessing and public celebration of marriage gave rise to a presumption that a clandestine union was illicit. It was a presumption however which admitted proof to the contrary, proof, namely, that there had been an exchange of true marital consent (" . . . *nisi voluntas propria suffragaverit et vota succurrerint legitima* . . . ")[58]

3. *Legislation Against Clandestine Marriages*

While secret marriages therefore were admittedly valid provided the exchange of consent could be established, the Church was severe in her legislation against them. Alexander III strictly forbade marriage to be celebrated secretly; and he decreed a suspension of three years for any preist who secretly blessed such a marriage.[59] At the Fourth Lateran Council, 1215, secret marriages were denounced, the banns of all marriages ordered to be published, and priests were directed to abstain from assisting at marriages which were not contracted publicly.[60] The Council had instituted the proclamations of banns as a means of eradicating the evil of secret marriages, and of thereby insuring the desired public celebration of marriage in a

[57] Berardi, C., *Gratiani Canones, Genuini ab apocraphis discreti*, p. II, T. I, pp. 41-43.

[58] Joyce, *Christian Marriage*, p. 104; Council of London, 1102, canon 22—Mansi, XX, 1152; c. 9, C. XXX, q. 5.

[59] Compilatio II, c. 2, *de clandestina desponsatione*, IV, 4.

[60] Canon 51; c. 3, X, *de clandestina desponsatione*, IV, 3.

fitting manner.[61] In England, France, Germany, and Spain, local and provincial Councils studied the question and attempted to legislate for it. Marriage must be celebrated with reverence and in the presence of the priest and witnesses; [62] no lay person (the Fürsprecher), may dare to assist at a marriage; [63] parties guilty of contracting secret marriage were threatened with excommunication; [64] or forbidden to approach the sacraments; [65] priests were forbidden to assist at such marriages at all; [66] and in some instances they were threatened with a suspension from office for three years if they violated the prohibition.[67]

Such were some of the laws passed in an effort to stem the rising tide of secret marriages. A stronger measure however was necessary, if these evils were to be checked with greater effectiveness and that measure was a substantial form of marriage. Several centuries were to pass before the desired reform was to be achieved. When the Fathers of the Council of Trent gathered for deliberation, this serious question of clandestine marriage was bound to arise.

[61] Esmein, *Le Mariage dans Le Droit Canonique*, 2 ed., I, 203.

[62] Synod of Salzburg, 1291—Mansi, XXIV, 1075; Provincial Council of Aranda, 1473—Hefele-Leclerque, *Histoire des Conciles*, VIII, 47.

[63] Synod of Trevers, 1227—Mansi, XXIII, 29; Council of Salzburg, 1420—Mansi, XXVIII, 1013; Council of Magdeburg, 1370—Mansi, XXVI, 402.

[64] Prov. Synod of Arles, 1255—Mansi, XXIII, 1001; Constitutions of Bourdeaux, 1263, c. 5—Mansi, XXIII, 1110; Council of Cologne, 1280, c. 10—Mansi, XXIV, 356; Council of Cahors, 1289, c. 18—Mansi, XXIV, 1012; Council of Padua, 1351—Mansi, XXVI, 234.

[65] Council of Padua, 1351—Mansi, XXVI, 234; Council of Salzburg, 1490—Mansi, XXXII, 505.

[66] Provincial Council of Scotland, 1225, c. 65—Mansi, XXII, 1241; Provincial Council of Salzburg, 1490—Mansi, XXXII, 505.

[67] Council of Prague, 1355—Mansi XXVI, 402; Council of Cahors, 1289, c. 18—Mansi, XXIV, 1012.

CHAPTER II

THE CELEBRATION OF MARRIAGE FROM THE COUNCIL OF TRENT TO THE CODE

THE Council of Trent reassembled under Pius IV, on January 4, 1562, after a long interruption,[1] and the question of a reform in clandestine marriages was proposed at one of the first minor sessions, March 11, 1562.[2] It was not until July 20, 1563, however, that the first draft for such reform was presented to the General Council for discussion.[3] While the seriousness of the evils of clandestine marriages was fully realized by all the Fathers present, it was quite evident from the very beginning that the question of reform was not to be settled quickly. It was feared that opposition would be too intense if the proposed decree for a reform in clandestine marriages were presented as a dogmatic canon. Hence it was placed as a disciplinary chapter which followed the dogmatic canons on marriage.[4]

ARTICLE I. THE DECREE "TAMETSI"

1. *The Debate in the Council*

In the first draft the decree on clandestine marriages proposed that in the future marriages which were contracted secretly and without three witnesses should be declared invalid and null.[5] The majority of the Fathers were in favor of this proposal. Some sixty, however,—among whom were several of the ablest and most eminent

[1] Pastor, *The History of the Popes,* XV, 264.

[2] Le Plat, *Monumentorum ad historiam Concilii Tridentini Amplissima Collectio,* t. V, 104.

[3] *Conc. Tridentini Diariorum, Actorum, Epistolarum, Tractatuum Nova Collectio,* IX, 639.

[4] Pallavicinus, *Hist. Conc. Trident.,* XXII, c. 4, n. 2.

[5] "Sacrosancta Dei Ecclesia statuit et decernit ea matrimonia quae in posterum clam non adhibitis tribus testibus contrahuntur irrita fore et nulla . . . " —*Conc. Tridentini Diariorum . . . Nova Collectio,* IX, 640.

Fathers, also the legate of the Pope, Hosius—were strongly opposed to it.[6] They declared that it was not within the sphere of the Church's authority to declare clandestine marriages invalid, because such marriages contained the essential elements of the sacramental sign, and to place a condition necessary for the validity of same, would be to introduce a change in the matter and form of the sacrament. Moreover, they argued, the evils of clandestine marriages were known for centuries, and yet, the Church never presumed to declare marriages null and void on account of them. Lainez turned the attention of the Fathers to the situation which would arise if heretics and even Catholic nations refused to submit to the new law on clandestine marriages. A situation worse than the present would result, he feared, for there would be endless discussions and doubts concerning legitimacy, hereditary succession, and likewise innumerable occasions of sin.[7]

On the other hand, those who were in favor of a decree to declare clandestine marriages null and void, were not united in their explanation of the authority of the Church to pass such legislation. Some distinguished between the contract of marriage, and the sacrament of marriage, and said that the Church in the decree did not legislate concerning the matter and form of the sacrament, but simply laid down an essential condition for the proper entrance into the contract.[8] Others argued for the lawfulness of the new decree from a comparison with the Church's authority in establishing other impediments, as for example, the impediment of age, consanguinity, affinity and the like. If the Church could attach invalidating effects to such factors, making them thereby diriment impediments to marriage, it was equally within her authority to lay down conditions which would govern the valid exchange of matrimonial consent.[9] A third group went even further, and asserted the authority of the Church to modify the sacramental sign[10]

[6] Pastor, *The History of the Popes*, XV, 339, 344.

[7] *Conc. Tridentini Diariorum . . . Nova Collectio*, IX, 645, 648; Pallavicinus, *Hist. Conc. Trident.*, XXII, c. 4, n. 8, 13, 25; c. 8, n. 18.

[8] *Conc. Tridentini Diariorum . . . Nova Collectio*, IX, 654.

[9] *Conc. Tridentini Diariorum . . . Nova Collectio*, IX, 644.

[10] *Conc. Tridentini Diariorum . . . Nova Collectio*, IX, 704, 706, 725.

The debate was carried on for several months, and the original draft was altered three times. On August 7, 1563, a second draft was presented in which persons were declared incapable of contracting marriage who in the future attempted to celebrate marriage without at least three witnesses.[11] On September 5, 1563, a double *schema* was proposed; the one was similar to that of August 7th; the other introduced a new note, for it prescribed a special quality for one of the witnesses, namely it called for the marriage to be celebrated before the parish priest, or a priest delegated by him or the Ordinary.[12] This fourth draft, which was again proposed on October 13, 1563.[13] contained the first mention of the *priest* as one of the required witnesses. It is somewhat surprising to note that the Fathers of the Council did not have the priest in mind from the beginning of their discussion. After the reading of the first draft the Cardinal of Lorraine requested that the priest be included among the witnesses, but his request was not immediately granted.[14] The objection to the priest at first was that four witnesses would be too severe a requirement upon the persons wishing to marry. Yet it was realized that unless there was an obligation resting upon one of the witnesses to record the marriage properly the entire purpose of the reform would be lost. Hence the discussion turned to the consideration of a stable and authoritative witness. Should a notary (*scriba*) or a priest be designated? For this capacity, it was pointed out that a notary was not suitable. There were so many of them, and it was understood that they might be easily deceived by the parties about their freedom to marry; or if not deceived, it was not improbable that they might be induced to assist unlawfully at forbidden marriages. It was felt on the other hand that

[11] "Sancta Synodus statuit ac decernit omnes illas personas quae in posterum clam sine trium saltem testium praesentia matrimonia . . . contrahere attentaverint, ad matrimonium . . . sic contrahenda inhabiles fore . . . "—*Conc. Tridentini Diariorum . . . Nova Collectio,* IX, 683

[12] " . . . inhabiles, sunt illi qui aliter quam praesente parocho, vel alio sacerdote de ipsius parochi seu Ordinarii licentia et duobus vel tribus testibus matrimonia contrahere attentaverint . . . "—*Conc. Tridentini Diariorum . . . Nova Collectio,* IX, 761-763.

[13] *Conc. Tridentini Diariorum . . . Nova Collectio,* IX, 889, 890.

[14] *Conc. Tridentini Diariorum . . . Nova Collectio,* IX, 642, 643.

the priest would make a far better official witness. His knowledge of Church law and the requirements for marriage would aid him in determining the freedom of the parties, and he could be relied upon to attend to proper registration of the marriage. Finally, however, it was decided that the priest should be included as one of the witnesses in whose presence marriage had to be celebrated in order to be valid. His role, however, from the point of view of valid assistance required only that he be able to attest to the exchange of consent. The Fathers were very reluctant to enlarge his authority, or to encroach in any way upon the liberty of the persons who desired to marry. The fourth draft, therefore, made explicit mention of the parish priest.[15]

The proposed reform of clandestine marriages was opposed until the very end. Pope Pius IV had written his legates that he favored all the reforms, and it can be presumed that his approval extended to the decree under discussion.[16] The final vote showed that the majority of the Fathers were in favor of the decree, while some fifty or more were against it. Of those opposed, several remitted their decision to the Holy Father.[17]. The decree, therefore, which was adopted by the Council of Trent in its twenty-fourth session, November 11, 1563, received Papal approval together with the other decrees of the Council, January 26, 1564.[18] To the world this decree has been known by the first word of its opening sentence, namely, the decree *Tametsi.* A summary of it is here given:

> Although it is not to be doubted that clandestined marriages made with the free consent of the contracting parties are valid and true marriages, so long as the Church has not rendered them invalid; and, consequently, that those persons are justly to be condemned, as the holy Synod doth condemn them with anathema, who deny that such marriage are true and valid; . . . nevertheless, the holy Church of God has for reasons most just, at all times detested and prohibited such marriages; . . . *those who shall attempt to contract*

[15] Pallavicinus, *Hist. Conc. Trident.*, XXII, c. 8, n. 16, 17.

[16] Le Plat, *Monumentorum ad historiam Concilii Tridentini Amplissima Collectio,* t. VI, p. 166.

[17] Pallavicinus, *Hist. Conc. Trident.*, XXIII, c. 9, n. 5.

[18] *Conc. Trident. Diariorum . . . Nova Collectio,* IX, 1152.

> *marriage otherwise than in the presence of the parish priest, or of some other priest by permission of said parish priest or of the Ordinary, and in the presence of two or three witnesses; the holy Synod renders such wholly incapable of thus contracting, and declares such contracts invalid and null, as by the present decree It invalidates and annulls them.*[19]

Thus was finally accomplished a reform which was long desired. In the past, as has been seen, attempts were made to check the evils of clandestine marriages, but they had not succeeded, partly because they were only local, and partly because they did not touch the real difficulty. In the decree *Tametsi* there were contained all the means for an effective reform. In actuality also it did much to check the evil with which the Church had contended for centuries. It may be safely said, however, that the effectiveness of this reform would have been far greater had it not been for the method which was chosen by the Fathers of the Council of Trent for the promulgation of this law.

2. *The Promulgation of the Decree Tametsi*

The decree *Tametsi* was to be published several times during the first year of its existence, but was not to be effective in any locality until thirty days from the day it was first published.[20] It was expected that as a matter of course the decree would be published throughout the world. For some reason or other, however, this did not take place. It was never published in many parishes, dioceses, and even entire nations refused to accept it; hence, the

[19] *Conc. Trident. Diariorum . . . Nova Collectio*, IX, 968, 969; Waterworth, *The Canons and Decrees of the Sacred and Oecumenical Council of Trent*, p. 196.

[20] "Ne vero haec tam salubria praecepta quemquem lateant ordinariis omnibus praecipit, ut cum primum potuerint curent hoc decretum populo publicari, ac explicari in singulis suarum dioecesium parochialibus ecclesiis, idque in primo anno quam saepissime fiat, deinde vero quoties expedire viderint. Decernit insuper, ut huiusmodi decretum in unaquaque parochia suum robur post triginta dies habere incipiat a die primae publicationis, in eadem parochia factae, numerandos"—*Conc. Trident.*, sess. XXIV, *de ref. matrim.*, c. 1.

beneficial results that were intended were never realized in many places. In the localities where it was not published the pre-Tridentine conditions continued to prevail. The result was that instead of a universal practice regarding the validity of the marrage celebration, an unevenness and a diversity of method was found, which often rendered the situation serious, and gave rise to many doubts and anxieties.

The method of promulgation which the Fathers of the Council decided upon was very unusual, and perhaps without a parallel in the previous or the subsequent history of the Church.[21] This method may seem somewhat unintelligible to a person of the twentieth century. In order to understand why it did not seem usual when it was selected, one has but to recall that in the sixteenth century religious bodies professing diverse beliefs were frequently set off from each other by territorial limits. This is the same as saying that in a given territory there was not the mixture of religious beliefs as exists today. The saying, "*cuius regio eius religio*" frequently was a reality. With this point well in mind, it becomes less difficult to understand and appreciate the motive of the Council of Trent in selecting the manner of publication which it did for its decree on clandestine marriages. In the Council discussion, Lainez had pointed out the evils which would follow from the decree if accepted; *per se* it would have to be binding on heretics as well as on the faithful, but it was very evident that the heretics would refuse to accept the decree; consequently, their marriages would be invalid, children of their marriages would have to be considered illegimate, and finally there would be innumerable discussions and law-suits regarding the right of hereditary succession. Pallavicinus notes that this observation of Lainez impressed the Council very much and they gave it great consideration.[22] If the view which Pallavicinus takes of the promulgation of the decree is correct, it would seem that this unusual method of publication was adopted because it supplied a means of exempting heretics from the decree *Tametsi* without however, inserting any clause of exemption in the decree proper. Real-

[21] Creagh, *The Ne Temere Decree*, p. 9.

[22] Pallavicinus, *Hist. Conc. Trident.*, XXII, c. 4, n. 8, 13, 25.

izing the defined religious limits which then existed, the Fathers believed that the heretics would not permit the publication of the decree *Tametsi* in the territories in which they were already established in large numbers; and since the decree would remain unpublished in such territories, marriages contracted there would not come under the new law, and hence would be valid.[23]

The Council instructed the Bishop of the diocese to authorize the publication of the decree *Tametsi* within his diocese.[24] A pastor could not publish it in his parish without the consent of the bishop. If he presumed to do so without the necessary instruction, his act would be invalid, and consequently clandestine marriages in that parish would continue to be valid.[25] The decree was to be published *in every parish church* of each diocese, and it was to begin to be in force *in each parish* at the expiration of thirty days, to be counted from the day of its first publication in said parish. The promulgation, therefore, of the decree at a diocesan synod or even in the cathedral church for the entire diocese was not considered sufficient. Moreover, in order that the faithful might be fully aware of its content, the decree was to be published in the vernacular tongue. Promulgation of it in Latin only would not bring about the necessary manifestation of the will of the legislator and the faithful would not be obliged to observe the law. Lastly, the decree *Tametsi* was to be published as a decree of the Council of Trent, not as an episcopal law, or as a provincial regulation. If it were published as such the publication was considered ineffective.[26]

The decree *Tametsi* called for the marriage to be contracted *coram parocho,* and two witnesses. A literal interpretation of this phrase would seem to justify the opinion that a valid marriage might

[23] Pallavicinus, *Hist. Conc. Trident.*, XXII, c. 8, n. 10; Benedictus XIV, Const., *Paucis adhinc hebdomadis,* 19 March, 1758—*Fontes,* n. 447.

[24] Although according to the wording of the decree the Bishop of the diocese was empowered to publish the decree *Tametsi,* the Holy See later required that its permission be obtained before proceding to publication—Gasparri, *De Matrimonio,* 3 ed., n. 1048.

[25] Gasparri, *op. cit.*, n. 1048; Wernz, *Jus Decretalium,* IV, n. 159.

[26] Benedict XIV, *De Synodo Dioecesana,* lib. XII, c. V, n. 7; S. C. C., Russiae (*Archiep. Chievien.*), 2 December, 1628—*Fontes,* n. 2500.

take place before any parish priest.[27] From a time, however, which immediately followed the Council of Trent, jurisprudence took another view of the meaning of *coram parocho*, and interpretated it as the *parochus proprius*, the proper parish priest of either of the parties. He alone could validly assist or give delegation for the marriage. This current view of jurists eventually prevailed, and was finally consecrated by authentic declarations of the Holy See.[28] By the term parochus proprius was understood a priest in whose parish a person had a domicile; later a quasi-domicile in a parish was considered sufficient to make the pastor a *parochus proprius*. At first this was only a probable opinion with regard to quasi-domicile, but the Holy Office in 1867 recognized it as a means of obtaining a *parochus proprius*, and laid down conditions under which a quasi-domicile could be required.[29]

The part of the proper parish priest (*parochus proprius*) at the marriage celebration was simply that of an official witness of the Church. He did not exercise any power of orders or of jurisdiction, and his position was similar to that of a notary who is the official witness of the State in a legal transaction.[30] Provided, therefore, that the proper parish priest retained his title of pastor, he could always assist validly at marriage even though the bishop had forbidden him to assist; [31] likewise his assistance was valid even though he did not have the order of prieshood, or was irregular, excommunicated, suspended from office, or under interdict. In the decree *Tametsi* the

[27] Cronin, *The New Matrimonial Legislation*, pp. 101-150, where the author presents a very excellent discussion of the true mind of the Council of Trent in this regard.

[28] Urban VIII, Const., *Exponi*, August 14, 1627—*Bullarium Romanum*, XIII, 537; Benedict XIV, Const., *Paucis abhinc*, March 19, 1758—*Fontes*, n. 447; "Votum Consultoris," *A. S. S.*, XL (1907), 525.

[29] S. C. S. Off., litt. encyl., 7 January, 1867—*Coll. P. F.*, n. 1407; Costello, *Domicile and Quasi-Domicile*, p. 44 ss.

[30] Pallavicinus, *Hist., Conc. Trident.*, XXII, c. 4, n. 3, 12; Benedict XIV, *De Synodo Dioecesana*, lib. XIII, c. 22, n. 6; Gasparri, *De Matrimonio*, 4 ed., n. 932.

[31] Benedict XIV, *De Synodo Dioecesana*, lib. XIII, c. 23, n. 3.

only expressed qualification of the official witness was that he be a parish priest.[32]

It was not always easy to determine whether the decree *Tametsi* had been published in a particular diocese. If any authentic attestations of the publication were available, doubts could be quickly dispelled. At times, however, there were no records; then, worthy witnesses, bishop, pastor, reliable laity might give sufficient testimony to solve the doubt. The fact that the decree *Tametsi* was observed in a locality gave rise to a presumption in favor of promulgation.[33] Benedict XIV declared that the observance of the decree *Tametsi* could be introduced through usage, even though it had never been published in the locality where custom accounted for its observance.[34]

It is only natural to ask in what countries the decree *Tametsi* was actually published. Certain countries, as England, Scotland, Denmark, Sweden, Norway and the like never accepted it; strictly Catholic nations such as Italy, France, Spain, Poland, Hungary, Portugal as a rule saw to its publication. Authors have compiled various charts showing where the decree *Tametsi* was published, and where it was not.[35] There were omissions and errors however in the

[32] Conc. Trident., sess. XXIV, *de ref. matrimon.*, c. 1; Benedict XIV, *De Synodo Dioecesana,* lib. XII, c. 5, n. 2 ss.; Giraldi, *Expositio Juris Pontificii,* II, sect. 115, n. 19-28; Suarez, *De Censuris,* Disp. XI, § 1, n. 24; Feije, *De Impedimentis et Dispensationibus matrimonialibus,* 285, 286.

[33] S. C. C., 26 September, 1602—in Benedict XIV, *De Synodo Dioecesana,* lib. XIII, c. 5, n. 6: "Publicationem praesumi, ubi id decretum fuerit aliquo tempore in parochia tamquam decretum Concilii observatum."—On January 10, 1866, the Sacred Congregation of the Holy Office interpreted the meaning of "aliquo tempore"; "Decretum Conc. Trid., diu dicitur observatum tamquam eiusdem Concilii decretum, quando a tempore quod excedit hominum memoriam, in parochia vim legis obtinuisse compertum est, ita ut matrimonia contracta praeter formam a Tridentino praescriptam irrita semper habita fuerint"—*Coll. P. F.*, p. 1279.

[34] Benedict XIV, Const., *Paucis abhinc,* 19 March, 1758—*Fontes,* n. 447.

[35] Feije, *De Impedimentis et Dispensationibus Matrimonialibus,* n. 320; Gasparri, *De Matrimonio,* 3 ed. Allegatum VI, p. 438; *Catholic Encyclopedia,* "Clandestinity," Lehmkuhl, *Theologia Moralis,* II, 785; especially Leinz, *Die Ehevorschrift des Councils von Trient,* pp. 80-82; 93-98. Zitelli, *Apparatus Juris Ecclesiastici,* pp. 428-435.

most carefully prepared lists, and hence the best rule was that the parties should follow the practice of their own diocese.[36]

The Fathers of the First Plenary Council of Baltimore, 1852, were aware that the decree *Tametsi* had only been published in certain dioceses of the United States. It seemed best to them also that there be no universal publication of it for this country. Some Fathers even thought that the Holy See should be asked to abrogate the decree in the places where it had been formally published. This petition however, was not sent to the Holy See.[37] At the Second Plenary Council, it was again advised that the decree should not be published for the entire country. Moreover, the Holy See was asked to restrict the decree *Tametsi* to the province of New Orleans. The Holy See replied that it was by no means fitting that this request should be granted.[38] At the request of the Holy See the Third Plenary Council of 1884 made an investigation of the question of formal and virtual promulgation of the decree *Tametsi*.[39] A list of the places in which the decree *Tametsi* was published is to be found in the letter of the Bishops of the Third Plenary Council of Baltimore to the Cardinal Prefect of the Sacred Congregation for the Propagation of the Faith.[40] The decree was published in the province of New Orleans, in the province of San Francisco together with the territory of Utah, save that part which lies east of the Colorado River, in the province of Sante Fe, except the northern part of Colorado, in the diocese of Vincennes, in the City of St. Louis and the parishes of St. Genevieve, Florissant, and St. Charles of the same archdiocese, in Kaskaskia, Cahokia, French Village, and Prairie du Rocher, all situated in the diocese of Belleville.[41]

In the same letter the Bishops stated that the Benedictine Declaration [42] had been extended to the Archdiocese of New Orleans, the

[36] Feije, *op. cit.*, n. 320; Wernz, *Jus Decretalium*, IV, n. 162.

[37] *Conc. Plen. Baltimor.*, I, pp. 31-34.

[38] *Conc. Plen. Baltimor., Acta et Decreta,* II, t. V, n. 340; also Instr., III, ad VI, pp. 1, xx.

[39] Guilday, P., *History of the Councils of Baltimore,* pp. 261, 262.

[40] *Conc. Plen. Baltimor.*, III, *Acta et Decreta,* p. cvii.

[41] *Conc. Plen. Baltimor., III, Acta et Decreta,* pp. cviii-cix.

[42] *Cf.* Art. II of this chapter.

dioceses of Mobile, Little Rock, Natchez and Natchitoches; also to the province of San Francisco, and the territory of Utah; to the diocese of Vincennes, and in the Archdiocese of St. Louis to the places wherein the decree *Tametsi* had been published: likewise to the places of the diocese of Belleville where the decree *Tametsi* was in force. In this same letter the Bishops mentiond that the Benedictine Declaration had not been extended to the province of Sante Fe; and that its extension to the dioceses of San Antonio, Galveston, and Brownsville (of the province of New Orleans) was doubtful. They requested the Holy See that the Benedictine Declaration be extended to Sante Fe, and that its publication in the other dioceses be made certain. The answer of the Holy See stated that the Benedictine Declaration was extended for certain to the places where its publication was doubtful. It refused to grant the wish of the Bishops regarding Sante Fe. Hence the Benedictine Declaration was never extended to that province.[43]

Article II. The Subject of the Decree "Tametsi"

1. *The Subject in General*

A reading of authors who have devoted themselves to this question will reveal that there was much uncertainty concerning the subjects of the decree *Tametsi.* With regard to Catholics there were many doubts arising from the question of publication, and reception of the decree; or concerning the obligation of an individual to observe the decree in special circumstances. The decree was both *territorial* and *personal.* Within the confines of the place where it had been published, it had to be observed; and it followed a person who had a domicile or quasi-domicile in such a locality and obliged him even though he was in a locality when the decree had not been published; it maintained its hold upon him until he obtained a domicile of quasi-domicile in the place of non-publication.[44]

A special difficulty arose concerning the marriages of heretics.

[43] *Conc. Plen. Baltimor.,* III, *Acta et Decreta,* pp. cviii-cvix.

[44] Inst. S. C. S. Off.; 14 December, 1859, in Gasparri, *De Matrimonio,* 3 ed., n. 1066.

Were they bound to observe the provisions of the decree? Speaking *per se,* and of a place wherein the decree *Tametsi* had been formally published, it seems certain that they were obliged by it. The Fathers of the Council made no provision for their exemption, and unless expressly exempt, it is the teaching of the Church that all baptized persons are obliged by her laws.[45] The Sacred Congregation of the Council left no doubt about this in a reply of January 8, 1678: "*Haereticos quoque, ubi decretum est promulgatum, teneri talem formam observare, ac propterea etiam ipsorum matrimonia absque forma concilii, quamvis coram ministro haeretico, magistratus civili contracta, irrita et nulla esse.*" [46] In this question of heretical marriages great prudence was necessary. Pius VII warned against rigidity in their regard saying that it was not true or safe to assert indiscriminately that such marriages were invalid. Great care and caution had to be observed for it might easily happen that the decree *Tametsi* had not been rightly published for the heretics, or again, it may have fallen into desuetude; or even, if published in a locality, the heretics might not have been included. Wherefore, circumstances had to be examined, and in doubt the decision of the Holy See would afford the only norm of action.[47] Regarding heretical marriages there were many instances of responses given by the Holy See but the scope of this historical summary will not permit a study of them. It would constitute a special treatise in itself. There is one particular reply which requires at least a brief consideration because of its influence upon the subsequent history of the decree *Tametsi,* namely, the Declaration of Pope Benedict XIV given for the Federated States of Holland and Belgium.

[45] Benedictus XIV, *Bullaria Benedicti* XIV, tom. III, pp. 4, 14, 16; Benedict XIV, ep. *Singulare Nobis,* 9 February, 1749—*Fontes,* n. 394; S. C. de P. F., 26 June, 1820—*Coll. P. F.* n. 747, 748; Conc. Trident., sess. VII, *de bapt,* canons 7, 8; Leinz, *Die Ehevorschrift des Councils von Trient,* p. 6.

[46] *Coll. P. F.,* n. 149.

[47] Pius VII, ep., *ad Archiepiscopum Moguntinum,* 8 October, 1803, Appendix VI, in Marsalla, *De Impedimentis,* p. 404; Gasparri, *De Matrimonio,* 3 ed., n. 1181; Feije, *De Impedimentis et Dispensationibus Matrimonialibus,* n. 306, 309-311; Schulte-Richter, *Canones et Decreta Conc. Trid.,* p. 291, n. 162.

2. *The Benedictine Declaration*

In the Federated States of Belgium and Holland a state of affairs developed towards the end of the sixteenth century which created many serious difficulties concerning the binding force of the decree *Tametsi.* Philip II of Spain ordered that the decree of the Council of Trent against clandestinity be published in Belgium, at that time a Catholic country under Spanish dominion. Margaret of Parma, the Regent, had asked that the publication of the decree be delayed, and was supported in her request by the Bishops of the United Province of Belgium. Philip II refused and the decree *Tametsi* was accordingly promulgated.[48] As a result of strife and rebellion against Spanish rule, Belgium was joined to the northern provinces. The religious situation changed almost radically. The Catholic religion was proscribed and the administration of the Sacraments was forbidden. In place of the former Catholic belief, a new heretical sect arose.[49] With this change of the religious outlook, it became a problem whether heretics were still obliged to observe the law of the Council of Trent regarding the form of marriage.[50] Theologians of eminence were opposed in their views; Lessius, Ballarmine Pignatelli, Schmaltzgrueber, were among those who declared that the marriage of heretics in these countries were invalid unless the law of the Council of Trent was observed. Others,—and especially many German canonists—asserted that these marriages were valid, because the decree *Tametsi,* was not meant to be binding on heretics.[51] The Vicar Apostolic for Holland was informed by the Holy Office in 1671, that for the Holy Office to pronounce judgment was undesirable. The Holy Office stated that he should act as he judged expedient for souls. He directed the ecclesiastical authorities at Ghent and Antwerp to treat all heretical and mixed marriages as valid. From that time on the clergy made no demands on converts that their marriages be rectified, if they had been previously celebrated without the canonical form,[52]

[48] Benedictus XIV, *De Synodo Dioecesana,* lib. VI, c. 6, n. 2.

[49] Alzog, *Church History,* III, 382.

[50] Benedictus XIV, *op. cit.,* lib. VI, c. 6, n. 3.

[51] Schulte-Richter, *Canones et Decreta Conc. Trident.,* p. 317.

[52] Schulte-Richter, *op. cit.,* pp. 308, 309; 319; Joyce, *Christian Marriage,* p. 134; Leinz, *Ausdehnung Der Ehevorschrift des Concils von Trient,* p. 45.

The opinion of theologians at Rome, Benedict XIV remarks, was that the heretical marriages were invalid. He himself, however, did not share this belief while he was Secretary to the Sacred Congregation of the Council.[53]

While Benedict XIV was still Archbishop of Bologna, the Bishop of Ypres asked the Congregation of the Council for a definite norm to follow with regard to the marriages of heretics. A commission was appointed to investigate the problem. It was composed of the Secretary of the Congregation of the Council, and three Roman theologians. Their reports were published in the Acts of the Congregation of the Council for the year 1741.[54] Clement XII died before he could give any decision. He was succeeded by Benedict XIV, who immediately took up the question. He examined the opinions set forth by the theologians and consulted the Cardinals in Rome. On November 4, 1741, he issued a decree entitled: "*Declaratio SSmi D. N. Benedicti XIV cum instructione super dubiis respicientibus matrimonia in Hollandia et Belgio contracta et contrahenda,*" [55] which has been known to posterity simply as the *Declaratio Benedictina*. In this document the following answers were given concerning the marriages of heretics: (1) provided that there was no other canonical impediment, the marriages which heretics contracted with each other in the past without observing the form prescribed by the Council of Trent were valid and all such marriages henceforth will be valid; [56] (2) mixed marriages,—provided there be no other canonical impediment—in the same provinces were valid and, henceforth, will be considered valid, even though the form of marriage prescribed by the Council of Trent is not observed.[57] This Declaration settled a much disputed question,

[53] Benedictus XIV, *De Synodo Dioecesana,* lib. VI, c. 6, n. 4.

[54] Benedictus XIV, *op. cit.*, lib. VI, c. 6, n. 5.

[55] *Bullaria Benedicti XIV,* t. I, p. 111; Schulte-Richter, *Canones et Decreta Conc. Trident.*, p. 324.

[56] . . . Matrimonia in dictis Foederatis Provinciis inter haereticos usque modo contracta, quaeque in posterum contrahentur, etiamsi forma Tridentina praescripta non fuerit in iis celebrandis servata, dummodo aliud non obstiterit canonicum impedimentum pro validis habenda esse"—*Declaratio SSmi D. N. Benedicti XIV, Bullaria Benedicti XIV,* t. I, p. 111, § 2; *cf.* also *De Synodo Dioecesana,* lib. VI, c. 6, n. 6.

[57] *Ibidem,* § 3; *cf. De Synodo Dioecesana,* lib. VI, c. 6, n. 12.

and greatly influenced the later discipline of the decree *Tametsi*. As is evident from the title of this Declaration, it was given for the Federated States of Holland and Belgium.[58] In the succeeding centuries, the Holy See extended the Bendictine Declaration to other parts of the world,[59] but because of the extreme care which was necessary to determine whether the Benedictine Declaration could be applied to a particular locality the Holy See reserved to itself the extension of it.[60] From the number of countries to which the Benedictine Declaration had been extended, it can be seen that the Holy See was generous in granting extensions of this document. There was no need of the Benedictine Declaration except in places wherein the decree *Tametsi* had been formally published, and where there was at the same time a large number of heretics. *Per se,* the decree *Tametsi* affected heretics, but the Benedictine Declaration, extended to the locality by the Holy See, carried with it the exemption of heretics from the law; mixed marriages in such places were valid although gravely unlawful. It remains to find on what grounds the Benedictine Declaration exempted heretics from the force of the decree *Tametsi.*

According to Benedict XIV, the marriages of the heretics in the Federated Provinces of Holland and Belgium were valid because it seemed clear to him from many sources that the Fathers of the Council of Trent did not intend to bind heretics to this law when the heretics were already united and organized into a society with churches and ministers.[61] The validity of mixed marriages was ex-

[58] *Declaratio SSmi. D. N. Benedicti XIV*, § 4; *cf.* also Benedict XIV, *De Synodo Dioecesana,* lib. VI, c. 6, n. 13, 14.

[59] See the lists of these places in the following authors: Leinz, *Die Ehevorschrift des Concils von Trient,* pp. 93-97; Gasparri, *De Matrimonio,* 3 ed. Allegatum VI, p. 528; Schulte-Richter, *op. cit.,* p. 326, n. 177.

[60] S. C. S. Off., 1855, *ad epis . . . Perigieux*—Leinz, *Die Ehevorschrift des Concils von Trient,* p. 5; Perrone, *De Matrimonio Christiano,* II, 209-221; Feije, *De Impedimentis et Dispensationibus Matrimonialibus,* n. 308; Wernz, *Jus Decretalium,* IV, p. 254 with note (150).

[61]."Ex verissimis siquidem argumentis conjecturisque probatum est, Concilium Tridentinum, quum novum illud dirimens impedimentum constituit decretum suum ad ea Matrimonia non extendisse quae disceptationi a Nobis an. 1741 solutae occasionem dedere"—Benedictus XIV, Constitution, *Singuare*

plained by Pope Benedict XIV through the principle of the communication of exemption—a principle which was admitted at that time in civil law. The heretic, being declared exempt from the law of the form of marriage, communicated his exemption from the law to his Catholic consort and, hence, the mixed marriage was valid.[62] This principle was only admitted in regard to the form of marriage; not with regard to other impediments, such as age, disparity of cult, and the like. It does not follow from the nature of the marriage contract, but is admittedly a concession on the part of the legislator. Previous to the time of Benedict XIV, this principle was accepted by some, and rejected by others; when he adopted it, it was accepted by all.[63]

In explaining the juridical nature of the Benedictine Declaration, Wernz and Gasparri agree that while it was primarily an authentic declaration concerning the decree *Tametsi* in the United Provinces of Holland and Belgium, it contained, nevertheless, what might be termed a dispensation *ad cautelam* from the decree *Tametsi*, and a special concession regarding mixed marriages.[64] For the parts of the United Provinces wherein heretics were organized as a distinct society the Benedictine Declaration was a simple declaration that the Fathers of the Council did not intend to subject them to the decree. For other sections of the United Provinces, however, where *de facto* Catholicism prevailed and heretics were in the minority,[64] the Bene-

Nobis, 9 February, 1749—*Fontes*, n. 394; Wernz, *Jus Decretalium*, IV, p. 256, in note.

62 "... quoniam, cum conjugum alter, tum ratione loci, in quo habitat, cum ratione societatis, in qua vivit, exemptus sit a Tridentinae Synodi lege, exemptio qua ipse fruitur, alteri parti communicata remanet, propter individuitatem contractus, vi cuius exemptio, quae uni ex partibus competit, ad alteram, secundum etiam leges civiles, extenditur, eidemque communicatur"—Benedictus XIV, *De Synodo Dioescesana*, lib. VI, c. 6, n. 12.

63 Votum Consultoris, C. Lombardi, A. S. S., XL (1907), 558; Gasparri, *De Matrimonio*, 3 ed., n. 1167; Vlaming, *Praelectiones Juris Matrimonialis*, II, p. 177, note 2.

64 Wernz, *Jus Decretalium*, IV, p. 254, note 151; Gasparri, *De Matrimonio*, 3 ed., n. 1188; Votum Consultoris, in *A. S. S.*, VII (1878), 62, sq.

65 There were some localities in which Catholicism continued its supremacy, for in particular cases the Congregation of the Council had declared heretical marriages were invalid because of failure to conform with the law of the Council

dictine Declaration contained a dispensation (at least *ad cautelam*) from the common law. The principle of communication of exemption regarding mixed marriages was not universally accepted in ecclesiastical law but owes its existence to a special concession of Benedict XIV in his Declaration. This opinion of the nature of the Benedictine Declaration takes the middle way between those who consider it either as a simple declaration and nothing more [66] and those who explain it as dispensation or derogation of the law of the Council of Trent granted by the supreme authority of Pope Benedict XIV.[67]

3. *Dispensations From the Decree Tametsi*

Besides the Benedictine Declaration there were other decrees of the Holy See which granted a real dispensation in matters of clandestine heretical or mixed marriages or both. These decrees were given for countries and localities where the Tridentine law was certainly in force and binding upon heretics as well as Catholics. Thus, a dispensation validating all clandestine mixed marriages was granted for Ireland in 1785; for Hungary in 1841; for Russia and Russian Poland in 1844; for Georgia (in Asia, lying between the Black and Caspian Seas) in 1845; for Bavaria, in 1834.[68] These dispensations are not extensions of the Benedictine Declaration. The Benedictine Declaration referred primarily to heretical marriages and to mixed marriage only secondarily. From the terms of these documents they are given expressly and directly for mixed marriages. It was a probable opinion, however, that while these dispensations made no special mention of heretical marriage, such marriages were rendered valid by

of Trent concerning the canonical form. This fact is mentioned by Pope Benedict XIV in the preamble of his declaration, *Bullaria Benedicti XIV*, t. I, p. 111, 1.

[66] Feije, *De Impedimentis et Dispensationibus Matrimonialibus*, n. 308; Cronin, *New Matrimonial Legislation*, p. 275; Gennaro, *Breve Commento sul decreto Ne Temere*, p. 40.

[67] Schulte, *Handbuch des katolischen Eherechts*, n. 47; Scherer, *Handbuch des Kirchenrechts*, p. 213, note 226; p. 216, note 238.

[68] For these dispensations together with the documents in which they are contained, *cf.* Zitelli, *Apparatus Juris Ecclesiastici*, pp. 437, 438.

them.[69] On the 12th of January, 1890, Pope Leo XIII declared valid all the marriages of heretics contracted among themselves in Malta even though the form of the Council of Trent was omitted, He expressly stated, however, that mixed marriages *were invalid* if not contracted according to the decree *Tametsi*.[70] In this instance it is to be noticed that for the first time the principle of the communication of exemption is explicitly disallowed.[71] In the Apostolic Letter published on the 18th of January, 1906, by Pope Pius X the Tridentine law of clandestinity was extended to the whole of the German Empire, but both the marriages of heretics and mixed marriages were declared exempt from its operation.[72] Later, this privilege was extended to Hungary.[73]

From this brief presentation of the question of the subject of the decree *Tametsi* it can be readily seen how difficult and, in many instances, how uncertain the doctrine was. The question is of little interest today except from a historical point of view; yet it reveals a situation which was in need of correction. The Church moves slowly in the way of innovation or changes in her law and this was particularly true in the case of the law on clandestinity. Having been enacted in November, 1563, it was not until the year 1905 that there appear signs which indicate that preparations are in order which will bring about a change in the general legislation. It was in that year that the Sacred Congregation of the Council began to discuss plans for a modification of the decree *Tametsi*. This modification finally manifested itself in a new decree,—the *Ne Temere*—which remained in substantial accord with its forerunner, but was so framed as to meet the problems which had grown up with the enforcement of the former law.

[69] Cronin, *New Matrimonial Legislation*, pp. 275-283; Wernz, *Jus Decretalium*, IV, n. 163, note 122; Gasparri, *De Matrimonio*, 3 ed., n. 1190.

[70] S. C. Neg. Extra.—*A. S. S.*, XXV, 696, 697.

[71] Cronin, *op. cit.*, p. 277; Gasparri, *De Matrimonio*, 3 ed., n. 1190.

[72] Litt. Ap., *Provida*, Pius X, 18 January, 1906—*A. S. S.* XXXIX (1906), 81-84; *cf.* Chapter VII of this Dissertation.

[73] A. K. K. R., LXXXIX (1909), 717-724.

Article III. The Decree "Ne Temere"

The Canon Law regarding the form of marriage, as has just been described, could hardly be regarded as satisfactory. One serious drawback was the lack of universality, caused by the method of promulgation decreed by the Council of Trent. Entire nations were left unaffected by it, not to speak of the divergency of practice which sometimes occurred in the same diocese. Moreover, in places where the decree *Tametsi* had been formally published, jurisprudence had given an interpretation to it which caused innumerable doubts and anxieties.[74] It required for the validity of a marriage the presence of the *parochus proprius*. No other priest could validly assist at a marriage unless he had permission from the *parochus proprius* of at least one of the parties. This interpretation was the cause of much confusion and misunderstanding as it was often very difficult to ascertain who was one's *parochus proprius*. In theory he was the one in whose parish a person had a domicile or quasi-domicile; a simple rule, indeed, but as far as actual practice was concerned it was by no means easy to apply. The conditions required for the acquisition of a domicile or quasi-domicile were somewhat stringent and doubts frequently arose concerning their fulfillment. Once a doubt arose concerning domicile it caused at the same time a doubt concerning the right of a priest to assist validly at a marriage. So the practice of restricting the right of valid assistance to the *parochus proprius* called for some revision.

It is not surprising therefore that many Bishops asked the Holy See for a modification of the decree *Tametsi*.[75] At the Vatican Council it was requested that the decree be abolished and a return made to the pre-Tridentine practice.[76] Finally, the Holy See took cognizance of the need of a change, and on May 20, 1905, the Sacred Congregation of the Council directed that two canonists be asked to

[74] S. C. C., decr., *Ne Temere*, 2 August, 1907—*Fontes*, n. 4340.

[75] *Cf.* the request made by the Bishops of the United States that the decree *Tametsi* be restricted to the province of New Orleans—*Conc. Plen. Baltimor. II, Acta et Decreta*, t. v, n. 340.

[76] Martin, *Coll. Documentorum Conc. Vatic.*, p. 163; *Collectio Lacensis*, VII, 842.

present statements from which a decree might be drawn up which would modify the decree *Tametsi.* This new decree was to be framed, keeping in view four principles, (a) the assistance of a priest at a marriage should be entirely voluntary, (b) in every case the freedom from impediment should be clearly proved, (c) the presence of two or three witnesses, and of the Ordinary or the parish priest of the place of contract ought to be sufficient for validity, (d) the new decree should affect the marriages of Catholics throughout the world.[77] The Consultors who were asked to prepare the *vota* were Archbishop Sili, and Monsignor Lombardi; the former was the Grand Almoner of Pope Pius X, and the latter Professor of Canon Law in the Pontifical University of the Roman Seminary, and *Defensor Vinculi Matrimonialis.*[78] The Congregation of the Council on February 17, 1906, discussed the proposals of the two Consultors, and likewise a plan for a revision of the decree *Tametsi* which Archbishop DeLai had drawn up from his own study of the *vota* proposed by the Consultors.[79] At this meeting the Cardinals of the Congregation agreed upon the substance of a general formula which was to be incorporated into the future decree. Consultations in the meantime were held with the Commission which was at the work of codifying the Canon Law of the Church. A new draft of the decree was submitted to the Congregation of the Council, July 14, 1906, and, after much discussion and the addition of amendments, another revision of the law was ordered.[80] The proposed decree was again examined and discussed at another session of the Council and finally presented to the Holy Father and received his approval on August 2, 1907. It was then given to the Catholic world, and became effective on Easter Sunday, April 19, 1908.[81]

The Holy See spared no effort in its endeavor to make the new

[77] *Acta Sanctae Sedis,* XL (1907), 531.

[78] Cronin, *The New Marriage Legislation,* p. 23.

[79] *Acta Sanctae Sedis,* XL (1907), 564-567.

[80] At this session of the Congregation of the Council, Cardinal Vives y Tuto and the then Monsignor Gasparri were present as representatives of the Commission for the Codification of Canon Law—*Acta Sanctae Sedis,* XL (1907), 564-567.

[81] *Acta Sanctae Sedis,* XL (1907), 525.

decree meet the problems which had developed with the practical application of the decree *Tametsi.* "Surely there is in this history of the framing of the *Ne Temere* much that is calculated in a manner worthy of the lofty subject with which it deals and of the vast body of Christians whom it is to affect. It was not thrust upon the world thoughtlessly or precipitately. For over two years all that the Church can boast of ripe experience in intricate matrimonial cases, of thorough acquaintance with the history and application of law, of familiarity with local differences and difficulties, has gone to the fashioning of this latest product of her creative genius." [82]

In the present historical summary it is not proposed to examine the provisions of the decree *Ne Temere* in detail. For the scope of this dissertation it will suffice to note a few contributions which the decree *Ne Temere* made to the legislation of the Church on the form of marriage. First of all, the new decree extended law of the form of marriage to the entire Catholic Church. There would no longer be a question of whether the form of marriage was published in this parish, in this diocese or in this country. At one stroke the difference of discipline which had formally existed was brushed aside, and the legislation concerning the canonical form was published for the entire Church. Secondly, the decree *Ne Temere* simplified the rule for valid assistance at marriage. Henceforth territory would serve as a basis for valid assistance. Within the limits of his diocese an Ordinary could assist validly at all marriages; within the limits of his parish a pastor could validly marry everyone who came to him. The disturbing and exclusive right of the *parochus proprius* to assist validly at marriage was set aside. The decree *Ne Temere,* however, made provisions for lawful assistance and in this regard the *parochus proprius* was given special consideration. Finally, all preceding dispensations and extensions of the Benedictine Declaration was abolished by the decree *Ne Temere,* with the one exception of the Constitution *Provida* which had been given to Germany by Pope Pius X, and was later extended to Hungary.[83] These exceptions were abrogated later by the Code of Canon Law.[84]

[82] Creagh, *A Commentary on the Decree "Ne Temere,"* p. 21.

[83] S. C. C., *Romana et aliarum,* 1 February, 1908, ad IV—*Fontes,* n. 4344.

[84] 30 March, 1918—*A. K. K. R.,* XCIX (1919), 19.

The Code of Canon Law repeated substantially the provisions of the decree of *Ne Temere*.[85] The changes which it introduced and which are of importance in certain instances will be noted in the succeeding chapters on the legislation which today governs the juridical form of marriage.

[85] Canons 1094-1099.

PART II

LEGISLATION OF THE CODE

CHAPTER III

THE ORDINARY FORM OF MARRIAGE

Canon 1094. Ea tantum matrimonia valida sunt quae contrahuntur coram parocho, vel loci Ordinario vel sacerdote ab alterutro delegato et duobus saltem testibus, secundum regulas expressas in canonibus qui sequuntur et salvis exceptionibus de quibus in canon 1098 et 1099.

In these words the present law of the juridical form of marriage in the Catholic Church is summarily expressed. Only those marriages are valid which are celebrated in the presence of the parish priest, or local Ordinary, or a priest delegated by them, and at least two witnesses. In the canons which follow canon 1094 rules are laid down for the valid celebration of marriage (canon 1095) and for the lawful celebration of marriage (canon 1097). The persons who must observe the juridical form of marriage as stated above are mentioned in canon 1099. Instances in which the Church permits a departure from the general law requiring a priest and two witnesses and permits marriage before witnesses alone are treated in canon 1098. Careful directions are given in canon 1096 for delegation to assist at marriage. The scope of this chapter will be to determine the meaning and comprehension of the title "pastor" and "local Ordinary" for the persons who are included under these titles are those who are authorized to assist at marriage. Their authority is ordinary in the sense that it is attached to the office which they hold (canon 197, § 1). In this chapter it will be necessary also to examine the qualities required of the other witnesses referred to in canon 1094. Before approaching the division of this chapter it will be helpful to make a few preliminary remarks concerning the form of marriage in general and the act of assistance at marriage.

The failure to observe the form of marriage as prescribed by the Council of Trent in the places wherein the decree *Tametsi* had been published was classified under the old law as a diriment impediment to marriage and was known as the impediment of clandestinity.[1] The Code, however, makes no reference to clandestinity as a diriment impediment; the source of the invalidity of a formless marriage is to be found in canon 1094. Persons who, according to canon 1099, are subjects of the canonical form but who attempted marriage before a justice of the peace and the like, may have been free from impediments whether diriment or prohibitive, and may have exchanged what was objectively a true matrimonial consent; nevertheless, in the eyes of the Church, there was no marriage since the consent given was juridically inefficacious. It was not expressed in the prescribed canonical form. The Church, it is true, has no authority over the *natural value* of acts of the intellect or will; but she can legislate conditions which must be observed if such natural acts are to have juridical effects.[2]

Although the Church requires that marriages be celebrated in the presence of the priest, it must be carefully borne in mind that the parties themselves are the ministers of the Sacrament of Marriage.[3] The blessing which is given by the priest does not effect the marriage. The marriage is contracted when the mutual consent of the parties is expressed in reply to the interrogation of the priest. The priest declares the parties married and asks the blessings of God upon the union. The duty of the priest at marriage from the juridical point of view is to witness the exchange of consent of the parties and to witness that exchange of consent on behalf of the Church. Pope Benedict XIV calls the priest assisting at marriage the *testis auctorizabilis* of the Church.[4] In keeping with the same idea, Cardinal Gasparri compares the juridical assistance of the priest rendered

[1] Gasparri, *De Matrimonio*, 3 ed., n. 542.

[2] Wernz-Vidal, *Ius Canonicum*, V. n. 531; Cerato, *De Matrimonio*, n. 76; Cappello, *De Sacramentis*, III, n. 205; Aertnys-Damen, *Theologia Moralis*, II, n. 694.

[3] Benedict XIV, *De Synodo Dioecesana*, lib. VIII, c. 13, n. 3; Aertnys-Damen, *Theologia Moralis*, II, n. 626.

[4] "Parochus interest matrimonio tamquam testis auctorizabilis pro Ecclesia; . . . idcirco Parochi praesentiam voluit (Ecclesia) ut in illius probitate maximum veritatis fundamentum statueret"—*De Synodo Dioecesana*, lib. XIII, c. 23, n. 6.

at the marriage ceremony to the function of a public notary who witnesses a transaction on behalf of the State.[5]

In assisting at a marriage as the official witness of the Church the priest does not exercise any power of sacred orders, nor is his act an act of jurisdiction. In order to realize the truth of this one need but to recall the attitude of the Fathers of the Council of Trent with regard to the position of the pastor at marriage.[6] The pastor, as was mentioned above, is the official witness of the Church. The duty of a witness is of a passive nature, namely, to observe what takes place and to testify to it. Ecclesiastical jurisdiction implies action, direction, as it is a public power granted by Christ to His Church through a canonical mission of governing the baptized to the end of obtaining eternal life.[7] A priest could hardly be said to place an act of jurisdiction when he is forced to assist at a transaction and in which he takes no part other than to see what has taken place; yet the Sacred Congregation of the Council declared such assistance at a marriage sufficient for its validity.[8]

It is the opinion of the vast majority of canonists that the principles of canon 209 regarding supplied jurisdiction in common error and in positive and probable doubt of either law or fact may be applied to assistance at marriage.[9] The reason for this position is that while assistance at marriage is not an act of jurisdiction in the strict sense of the word, it resembles a jurisdictional act very closely. It is possessed in virtue of an office, *i. e.*, a pastorate, which is an office

[5] Gasparri, *De Matrimonio,* 4 ed., n. 932.

[6] Pallavicinus, *Hist. Conc. Trident.*, lib., XXII, c. 4, n. 3, 12. *Cf.* Chapter II, Art. I of this dissertation.

[7] Chelodi, *Ius de Personis,* p. 201; Maroto, *Institutiones,* II, n. 573.

[8] Benedict XIV, *De Synodo Dioecesana,* lib. XIII, c. 23, n. 1.

[9] S. C. C., March 10, 1770—Pallotini, vol. XIII, V. *Matrimonium,* XV, n. 90; Gasparri, *De Matrimonio,* 4 ed., n. 936; Wernz-Vidal, *Ius Canonicum,* V, n. 536; Payen, *De Matrimonio,* II, n. 1763; Cappello, *De Sacramentis,* III, n. 663; Noldin, *Theologia Moralis,* III, p. 664; Vermeersch-Creusen, *Epitome,* II, n. 392; Vlaming, *Praelectiones Iuris Matrimonialis,* II, n. 568; Wouters, *De Forma . . . Celebrationis Matrimonii,* p. 8; Chelodi, *Ius Matrimoniale,* n. 131; Trombetta, *Supplet Ecclesia,* pp. 23-25; *Periodica,* XXII (1933), 192*-196*; Kearney, *Principles of Delegation,* pp. 126, 127. To the contrary, Jone, *Theol.-Pract. Quartalschrift,* LXXXI (1928), 806 ss; Linneborn, *Grundriss des Eherechts,* ed. 1933, p. 350, note 2.

of jurisdiction. The Pontifical Commisson for the Interpretation of the Code stated that an assistant with general delegation for marriage may subdelegate. In doing this the Commission applied the general principles which govern the delegation of jurisdiction.[10] The Code of Canon Law itself in speaking of asistance at marriage uses words which apply to delegation, such as *delegatus* (canon 1094), and *delegatio* (canon 1096, § 1). It is this similarity that has prompted most writers to look upon assistance at marriage as an act of jurisdiction in a wide sense and apply to it the principles of canon 209 concerning supplied jurisdiction in a case of common error or in a positive and probable doubt of a pastor's right to assist. The general teaching of authors concerning the elements which must be present to constitute common error as well as the conditions giving rise to a positive and probable doubt of fact or law will of necessity have to be carefully verified before it can be said that jurisdiction has been supplied.[11] It is to be noted that supplied jurisdiction may be invoked either in common error, or positive and probable doubt; both need not be present.[12]

The pastor and local Ordinary received their authority to witness marriage from the common law in canon 1094. Accordingly, the Ordinary cannot directly deprive a pastor of this authorization. He may forbid the pastor to assist at a certain marriage but if the pastor should violate this order and assist at the marriage within his jurisdiction the marriage will be valid although unlawful and sinful.[13] The jurisdiction of the local Ordinary is coextensive with the limits of his diocese. He need not *per se* obtain the permission of a pastor to witness a marriage in his parish, for he can validly and lawfully assist at marriages within his jurisdiction. He may delegate another

[10] Pont. Comm. Interp., 28 December, 1927—*A. A. S.*, XIX (1928), 61 *Cf.* also canon 199, § 3.

[11] Aertnys-Damen, *Theologia Moralis*, II, n. 359 ss.

[12] Cappello, *De Sacramentis*, III, n. 664.

[13] Gasparri, *De Matrimonio*, 4 ed., n. 942; Vlaming notes that the assistance rendered would be invalid if the Pope had forbidden the pastor to assist, as he is above the common law—*Praelectiones Iuris Matrimonialis*, II n. 569, note 2; *cf.* also S. C. C. (1581), in Benedict XIV, *De Synodo Dioecesana*, lib. XII, c. 5, n. 2; also *ibid.*, lib. XIII, c. 23, n. 3.

priest to assist at a marriage anywhere within the limits of his diocese but it is generally understood and accepted that the local Ordinary will not exercise such authority regardless of the local pastor.[14]

With these preliminary remarks a direct consideration of canon 1094 may be taken up. This chapter will consist of three articles; the first, considering the meaning of the title "pastor" in regard to assistance at marriage; the second, treating of the extension of the term local Ordinary; and the third discussing the qualification and manner of assistance required of the other witnesses.

Article I. The Pastor

In virtue of canon 1094 the pastor is authorized to assist at marriage. It is all important, therefore, to appreciate the meaning of the title "pastor," and to determine those who are included in it as everyone who comes within its meaning is *de iure* authorized to assist at marriage. The valid and lawful exercise of this mandate will be discussed in a later chapter. The aim of the present article is to determine which ecclesiastics are included in the title "pastor."

In general it may be stated that the title pastor includes those who are pastors in the strict sense of canon 451, § 1, and those who in Church law are classified as equivalent to a pastor with all his rights and obligations (canon 451, § 2).

1. *Pastor in the Strict Sense*

Canon 451, § 1, defines a pastor as "a priest or moral person to whom a parish is entrusted with the care of souls, to be exercised under the authority of the local Ordinary." The office therefore of a pastor may reside in a physical or moral person; if the former, he must be an ecclesiastic endowed with the sacerdotal character, which is now a requisite for a pastorate (canon 453).[15] Sometimes by spe-

[14] Wernz-Vidal, *Ius Canonicum,* V. n. 541; Cappello, *De Sacramentis,* III, n. 649; Vlaming, *op. cit.,* n. 569.

[15] Under the Tridentine discipline a cleric could be a pastor, and hence assist at marriage. *Cf.* Gasparri, *De Matrimonio,* 3 ed., n. 1082; De Smet, *De Spons. et Matrimonio,* 4 ed., I, n. 107, note 2.

cial designation of the Holy See a parish is entrusted to the care of a religious community, or to a Cathedral Chapter, and the moral person is invested with the title of pastor. The actual care of such a parish, however, must be entrusted to a priest who is called a parochial vicar actual. He alone enjoys the authorization to assist at marriage *de iure;* not the members of the moral person.[16]

II. *Pastor in the Broad Sense*

In canon 451, § 2, two groups of priests are declared the equals of pastors; (a) quasi-pastors, and (b) parochial vicars who have full parochial authority. They have all the obligations and rights of pastors, and hence *de iure* assist validly at marriage.

A. QUASI-PASTORS. A quasi-pastor is a priest who has charge of a quasi-parish, which in turn is a territorial division of a Vicariate or Prefecture Apostolic with a determined group of faithful, a church and a pastor (canon 216, § 3).[17] A quasi-pastor must observe the laws laid down in canons 1095 and 1096 for the valid and lawful exercise of his mandate to assist at marriage.[18]

B. PAROCHIAL VICARS WITH FULL PAROCHIAL AUTHORITY. Classified as parochial vicars with complete parchial authority and hence the right to witness marriages are the following:

1. *Actual Vicar* of a parish which has been given to a moral person (canon 471, §§ 1, 4).

2. *Administrator of a vacant parish* (canon 472, n. 1; canon 473, § 1). Before an administrator is appointed to a parish which has become vacant through the death of the pastor, the senior assistant validly assists at marriages *de iure,* unless some other provision has been made (canon 472, n. 2).[19]

3. *Vicar Adjutant* (or *Vicarius Adjutor*), appointed by the Ordinary to help a pastor who is incapacitated, and unable to discharge

[16] Canon 452, §§ 1, 2, and canon 471, §§ 1, 4.

[17] Instr., S. C. P. F., 25 July, 1920—*A. A. S.*, XII (1920), 331 ss.

[18] *Ibid.*, n. 6, 7.

[19] If the assistants are of equal rank, the oldest will assume administration; if there are no assistants, the nearest pastor is to take charge of parochial affairs until an administrator is appointed (canon 472, n. 2).

his duties. A vicar adjutant may assist at marriages provided he has been commissioned by the Ordinary to assist the pastor in all his duties (canon 475, §§ 1, 2).

4. *Vicar Substitute.* There are several types of substitutes which must be carefully distinguished. A vicar substitute is a priest who is appointed to take charge of a parish when its pastor is to be absent legitimately for more than a week; or a priest who takes the place of a pastor who has been removed from his benefice but has appealed his case to the Holy See (canons 474 and 1923, § 3). In the case of a legitimate absence which is to last longer than a week, the pastor proposes the name of his substitute to the Ordinary for his approval; and if he is a religious he must have, moreover, the approval of his Superior (canon 465, § 4). If a pastor is called away suddenly for a grave reason (*repentina et gravi causa*) and will be obliged to be absent for more than a week, he will choose a vicar substitute and notify the Ordinary of his choice (canon 465, § 5). In the case of supply for a removed pastor (canon 1923, § 3) the choice will rest with the Ordinary. A vicar substitute supplies the pastor in the care of the parish in every respect unless the Ordinary or pastor reserves certain duties (canon 474). The general opinion of writers is that this authority of the vicar substitute is ordinary, because it is possessed in virtue of his office.[20]

Thus far attention has been directed only in general to the office and duties of a vicar substitute. It remains to consider him with special reference to assistance at marriage. A vicar substitute appointed to the parish of a removed pastor may assist at marriages unless the Ordinary limits his authority in this respect (canon 474). A vicar substitute supplying for a pastor who has gone for a week cannot validly assist at marriages until he has received the approval of the Ordinary. This has been the decision of the Commission for the Interpretation of the Code.[21] If he is a religious, however, he may assist at marriages once he has received the approval of the Ordinary, and prior to the approval of his Superior.[22] The same

[20] Cappello, *Periodica,* XIX (1930), 2*; Fanfani, *De Iure Parochorum,* n. 251; Matth. a Coronata, *Institutiones Iuris Canonici,* I, n. 490.

[21] 14 July, 1922—*A. A. S.,* XIV (1922), 527, 528, ad II.

[22] *Ibid.,* ad III.

Commission declared that a vicar substitute supplying for a pastor who had departed for a sudden and serious reason could assist at marriages from the moment of his appointment and could continue to do so until the Ordinary informed him to the contrary.[23] In these circumstances the pastor should advise the Ordinary of his selection, but should he fail to advert to this obligation, or if the letter were lost or never reached the Ordinary, the assistance rendered would be valid.[24]

What kind of approval is necessary for a vicar substitute of a pastor who is departing and will be gone for more than a week? Must it be explicit and given to a determined priest in each case? It seems that the Ordinary may give permission to pastors to call upon the Superior of a religious community in his diocese for priests to supply during their absence which is to be longer than a week. This would be a general approval of all the religious in a special house, and an approval in particular of the individual religious whom the Superior selects. The Code is silent on this point. It calls for the approval of the substitute (canon 465, § 4) but does not determine the manner of approval. It seems reasonable to interpret this approval as sufficiently verified in an antecedent and general approval as has been described.[25] It would appear that an assistant, who has not general delegation for marriage, may nevertheless be designated as a vicar substitute on the ground that he was already sufficiently approved by the Ordinary when he was sent to the parish to assist the pastor.[26] Likewise, if an Ordinary, perfectly aware of a custom which exists in his diocese whereby a pastor who is going away for over a week gives the charge of his parish to a neighboring pastor and said Ordinary does not legislate against this practice in the statutes of the diocese, it would seem that the neighboring pastor is approved sufficiently to be constituted as a vicar substitute of canon 465, § 4.[27]

If a pastor is to be gone for a few days only, canon 465, § 6, states

[23] *Ibid.*, ad IV.

[24] Cappello, *De Sacramentis,* III, n. 649.

[25] Cappello, *Periodica,* XIX (1930), p. 3*.

[26] *Jus Pontificium,* X (1930), 341, 342.

[27] *L'Ami du Clergè,* 5 series, n. 48 (1933), 800.

that he must provide for the spiritual care of his parishioners especially when particular circumstances warrant it. A priest who takes care of the parish in this interval is not a vicar substitute, nor is he (it is presumed at present) an assistant with general delegation for marriage. Canon 1096, § 1, prohibits general delegation except to assistants, and hence he cannot be generally delegated to take care of any marriages which may turn up. If the pastor is delayed longer than a week the priest in charge would then become a vicar substitute and equivalent to the vicar substitute of a pastor who has been forced to depart suddenly for grave reason and accordingly may assist at marriage. The pastor in the meanwhile should notify the Ordinary of his delay, and the appointment of the vicar substitute.[28] Hence the priest supplying for a few days according to canon 465, § 6, cannot assist at marriages in general but must be delegated expressly for each marriage.

At this point it may be asked whether an assistant (*vicarius cooperator*) may assist at marriage solely in virtue of his office. Canon 476, § 6, states that the rights and obligations of an assistant are to be gathered from the diocesan statutes, the letter of the Ordinary, and the disposition of his pastor. This same canon continues with the following words: "*sed, nisi aliud expresse caveatur, ipse debet ratione officii parochi vicem supplere eumque adiuvare in universo paroeciali ministerio, excepta applicatione Missae pro populo.*" These words, a few writers argue, indicate that *per se* an assistant in virtue of his office is to supply the pastor in the entire ministry of his parish and this certainly includes assistance at marriage. Any restriction of this authority, according to their view, must be made by diocesan statutes, the letter of commission from the Ordinary, or by the pastor of the parish to which he has been assigned.[29] On the contrary, however, most canonists agree that an assistant does not assist at marriage in virtue of his office. In other words, his authority to witness marriage is not ordinary.[30] If an as-

[28] Cappello, *Periodica,* XIX (1930), 5*.

[29] Fanfani, *De Iure Parochorum,* n. 308; Krüger, *Die Delegation zur Eheassistenz—Apollinaris,* V (1932), 493-497; *Jus Pontificium,* XIII (1932), 307-311.

[30] Gasparri, *De Matrimonio,* 4 ed., n. 935, n. 5; Wouters, *De Forma . . . Celebrationis Matrimonii,* p. 25; Wernz-Vidal, *Ius Canonicum,* V, p. 633, note

sistant had ordinary power to witness marriages, canon 1096, § 1, would be without meaning, for by it general delegation is prohibited except to assistants for the parish to which they are assigned. Likewise, the controversy which lasted for several years as to whether assistants may subdelegate when they have already received general delegation would have been meaningless, for canon 199, § 1, clearly indicates that one with ordinary power may delegate, unless expressly forbidden. The reply of the Commission of Interpretation which stated that assistants with general delegation may subdelegate took it for granted that assistants did not possess ordinary power to witness marriage.[31] To the above observations may be added the fact that assistance at marriage is enumerated by the Code as a function which is expressly reserved to the pastor (canon 462, n. 4). The phrase *"nisi aliud expresse caveatur,"* etc., upon which the advocates of the opposite view place their argument ought to be explained in the light of the facts just mentioned, namely, that the assistant in virtue of his office (*ratione officii*), may be designated to assist the pastor in the entire ministry of the parish but the actual extent of his rights and obligations will be determined by diocesan statutes, his letter of appointment, and the will of his pastor. Hence it is that an assistant alone, as canon 1096, § 1, states, can receive general delegation for marriage. It is this potentiality which distinguishes an assistant as such from other priests who come to offer their services to the pastor for a time only. According to Gasparri there is only one case in which an assistant may be given full *parochial authority* (which *ipso facto* would include assistance for marriage) and that is in the event that he were given charge of a mission church of the parish which was at a great distance from the parish church.[32]

The general mandate of canon 1094 embraces also personal pas-

43; De Smet, *De Spons. et Matrimonio,* 4 ed., I, 107, note 3. De Becker, *De Matrimonio,* p. 139; Vlaming, *Praelectiones Iuris Matrimonialis,* II, n. 564; Cappello, *De Sacramentis,* III, n. 674; Vermeersch-Creusen, *Epitome,* II, n. 391; Chelodi, *Ius Matrimoniale,* n. 133, note 2; *Apollinaris,* V. (1932), 493-497.

[31] Pont. Comm. Interp., 28 December, 1928—*A. A. S.,* XX (1928), 61, 62, ad I.

[32] Gasparri, *De Matrimonio,* 4 ed., n. 935, n. 5; *cf.* also S. C. C. *in causa Principis Alberten et Saskatoonen*—*A. A. S.,* XXV (1933), 436-438.

tors. In the following chapter the meaning of a personal pastor and the extent of his authority will be discussed more at length. Hospital chaplains and priests in charge of other charitable institutions such as orphanages, homes for the aged and infirm, and the like, have authority to witness marriages only when they have been established in their respective institution *with full parochial rights.* Whether they have such authority is a question of fact and will have to be determined from the particular regulations which the Ordinary has issued for these places.[33] While the Rector of a seminary is exempt from parochial jurisdiction, he does not possess any authority *de iure* to witness marriage (canon 1368).

A putative pastor, namely, one who is believed to be a pastor while *de facto* he is not, may validly assist at a marriage because the Church will supply the needed authority in common error (canon 209). Likewise in a positive and probable doubt of law or fact concerning the pastor's right to assist, or the expiration of a general delegation, a pastor or priest may assist. The Church will supply the necessary authority.[34] Pope Pius VI in his instruction to the Gallican Bishops declared that marriages contracted before a *parochus intrusus, i. e.,* one appointed to a pastorate by an incompetent authority, as was done by civil authorities in France towards the end of the eighteenth century, were invalid.[35] However, since no special title is required by the Code as a basis of common error, under the present law it may be possible to have a case of common error even though a pastor is a *parochus intrusus.*[36]

Article II. The Local Ordinary

The Code of Canon Law clearly defines the extension of the term "local Ordinary" and accordingly all who come within its meaning

[33] S. C. C., *Romana et aliarum,* 1 February, 1908, ad X—*Fontes* n. 4344; Wernz-Vidal, *Ius Canonicum,* V. 533 (b) and (c); Cappello, *De Sacramentis,* III, n. 668; Wouters, *De Forma . . . Celebrationis Matrimonii,* p. 7.

[34] Before the Code of Canon Law the validity of assistance in a case of common error was admitted, but a *titulus coloratus* was required. *Cf.* Gasparri, *De Matrimonio,* 3 ed., n. 1082; such a title is not required by the Code—Cappello, *op. cit.,* III, n. 663.

[35] Gasparri, *De Matrimonio,* 4 ed., n. 938.

[36] Cerato, *De Matrimonio,* n. 92; Cappello, *De Sacramentis,* III, n. 661.

are empowered by canon 1094 to assist at marriage. Besides the Roman Pontiff, the following are classed as local Ordinaries; residential Bishops, Abbots and Prelates *Nullius,* and Vicars General of all three; Administrators, Vicars and Prefects Apostolic;[37] and finally those who by law or approved constitutions succeed the aforementioned during a vacancy or other impediment to office, viz., the Chapter of the Cathedral (canon 431), Abbacy, or Prelature (canon 324), before the election of a Vicar Capitular (canon 435); and in mission countries, the Pro-Vicar and Pro-Prefect Apostolic (canon 309, § 2). In the dioceses of the United States, the functions of the Chapter and Vicar Capitular are fulfilled respectively by Diocesan Consultors and the Administrator of the vacant diocese.[38]

The Roman Pontiff is the Ordinary Pastor of the Universal Church, according to the definition of the Vatican Council, and has, therefore, the right to assist at marriages of the faithful in any part of the world.[39] Leo XII stated this expressly in his apostolic letter to the Swiss, October 4, 1828.[40] A Vicar-General can assist at marriage anywhere in the diocese. His authorization ceases when the Bishop dies, resigns, or otherwise vacates his diocese. The Board of Consultors may assist at marriage before the appointment of an administrator, but must do so collectively, or through a delegate. Individual members of the board are not authorized for marriage. In assisting in a body the entire board would only represent the official witness and, according to the law, two additional witnesses would be necessary.[41] It was believed that a Legate of the Holy See could assist at marriage within the confines of his territory.[42] They cannot assist under the present law, however, for they are not classi-

[37] Vicars and Prefects Apostolic are not allowed to appoint Vicars General. They may, however, appoint Vicars Delegate who enjoy all the powers of jurisdiction which the Vicar or Prefect Apostolic has excepting those which the Vicar or Prefect reserves to himself, or which by law require a special mandate. (S. C. P. F., litt. 8 December, 1929—*A. A. S.*, XII, 1920, 120.)

[38] Canon 427; III *Plen. Conc. Balt.*, II, c. 2, n. 18—*Acta et Decreta Conc. Plen. Balt.*, III, p. 14.

[39] Sess., IV, cap. 3—*Coll. Lacensis,* vol. VII, col. 271.

[40] Gasparri, *De Matrimonio,* 3 ed., n. 1117.

[41] Cronin, *New Matrimonial Legislation*, p. 64.

[42] Lehmkuhl, *Theologia Moralis,* II, n. 776.

fied in the Code as Ordinaries.[43] Gasparri remarks that the Apostolic Delegate usually receives this authority in his letters of commission.[44]

With the exception of Cardinal Bishops, Cardinals are not Ordinaries, and hence are not authorized *de iure* to assist at marriage.[45] Formerly when Cardinals possessed quasi-episcopal jurisdiction over the clergy and people of their titular Church, it was believed that they could assist as an Ordinary at marriages celebrated in their titular Churches. Innocent XII reduced the jurisdiction of Cardinals to what is called *iurisdictio domestica* and transferred quasi-episcopal jurisdiction to Cardinal Vicar of Rome.[46]

Article III. The Witnesses

In addition to the parish priest or Ordinary, the marriage must be celebrated in the presence of at least two other witnesses. In this requirement the Code only renews the provisions of the former decrees, both the *Ne Temere* and the *Tametsi*.[47] The witnesses other than the parish priest are frequently referred to as "common witnesses" to distinguish them from the parish priest himself and Ordinary who are "qualified witnesses." The distinction has its source in the capacity in which the priest is present at a marriage as distinct from that of the other witnesses. He represents the Church and his testimony is accepted as official. In this present article the qualifications of the common witnesses alone will be discussed. The duties of the priest at marriage will be taken up in another chapter.

With reference to the number of common witnesses required, it is clear from the canon that there must be at least two. There may be many more, but never less. The Sacred Congregation of the Coun-

[43] Wernz-Vidal, *Jus Canonicum,* V, p. 627, note 27; Cappello, *De Sacramentis,* III, n. 651.

[44] Gasparri, *De Matrimonio,* 4 ed., n. 941.

[45] Gasparri, *op. cit.,* n. 940; Wernz-Vidal, *loc. cit.*

[46] Const., *Romanus Pontifex,* Innocent XII, 17 September, 1692—Gasparri, *op. cit.,* n. 940; Cronin, *New Matrimonial Legislation,* pp. 65, 66.

[47] Conc. Trident., sess. XXIV, *de ref. matrim.,* c. 1; S. C. C., decret., *Ne Temere,* 2 August, 1907, Art. III—*Fontes,* n. 4340.

cil has ruled that this number is necessary for the validity of the marriage and declared a marriage with one witness as invalid even though the parties were in good faith.[48]

As regards special qualifications in the common witnesses it is to be noted that the Code has very carefully refrained from requiring any. In doing this it followed the example of the framers of the decree *Tametsi*, and the decree *Ne Temere*. Pallavicinus relates that the Fathers of the Council of Trent deliberately avoided requiring any special qualities in the witnesses to the marriage contract in order to check any possible doubts or anxieties about marriages due to the proper qualifications of the witnesses.[49] The only requisites of a common witness to a marriage, therefore, are the use of reason and ability to testify to the marriage.[50] Accordingly, men, women, children, priests, secular as well as religious, nuns, heretics, infidels and excommunicates—all may *validly* act as common witnesses provided they have the use of their faculties and can testify to what takes place.[51] Hence insane persons, persons completely intoxicated, and children who have not obtained the use of reason cannot validly act as common witnesses. There is no provision in the Code which regulates how common witnesses are to be chosen, or how they are to witness the marriage. They will assist validly, therefore, even if forced to do so by fear or violence. Likewise, their assistance would be valid even if they are unaware of their position as witnesses provided only that they perceive in such a manner as to testify that a marriage has taken place.[52]

[48] S. C. C., 14 January, 1673—Schulte-Richter, *Canones Conc. Trident.*, p. 227, n. 40; Benedictus XIV, *De Synodo Dioecesana*, lib. XII, c. V, n. 5; Gasparri, *De Matrimonio*, 3 ed., n. 1155.

[49] *Hist., Conc. Trid.*, lib. XXII, c. 4, n. 12.

[50] Leitner, *Katholisches Eherechts*, p. 192; Gasparri, *De Matrimonio*, 4 ed., n. 961; Vlaming, *Praelectiones Iuris Matrimonialis*, II, n. 576; Benedictus XIV, *De Synodo Dioecesana*, lib. XII, c. 5, n. 5.

[51] Chelodi, *Ius Matrimoniale*, n. 131; Cappello, *De Sacramentis*, III, n. 654; Gasparri, *op. cit.*, 963; Wernz-Vidal, *Ius Canonicum*, V, n. 540.

[52] Cappello, *De Sacramentis*, III, n. 652, 653; Vlaming, *Praelectiones Iuris Matrimonialis*, II, n. 577; Gasparri, *De Matrimonio*, 4 ed., n. 963; De Smet, *De Spons. et Matrimonio*, 4 ed., I, n. 123, note 2; Wouters *De Forma . . . Celebrationis Matrimonii*, p. 15.

Thus far only the valid assistance of common witnesses has been discussed. Reverence for the sacrament demands that the greatest care be exercised in the selection of suitable witnesses. Diocesan statutes will frequently exclude certain persons. In general, it may be said that non-Catholics, public sinners, and excommunicates may not lawfully act as common witnesses.[53] Vermeersch would admit an excommunicated person to the position of a common witness, because it is not enumerated among the legitimate acts which one cannot exercise if he is excommunicated.[54] With regard to heretics, the Holy Office has declared in a particular reply that they should not be taken as witnesses for marriage, yet, the Ordinary may permit them to act as witnesses if there is a just reason and no scandal will ensue.[55]

The assistance rendered by the priest and that of the common witnesses must be simultaneous, which is to say, they must all be present for the same marriage. The law is clear on this point . . . *coram parocho et duobus saltem testibus.*[56] Priest and common witnesses must be physically present. It is generally accepted that equivalent presence which is achieved by the use of a telephone will not satisfy the presence required by the law.[57] Mere physical presence (or material presence), however, will not suffice for the validity of the marriage. The common witnesses must be present in an intelligent manner (*humano modo*). They must perceive that a marriage is taking place and that the parties have exchanged consent.[58]

The priest who is assisting at the marriage should see to it that the parties express their consent in a loud, clear, voice so that the witnesses may hear it properly. Consent is normally to be expressed in words but for validity the Code recognizes consent which is ef-

[53] Cappello, *De Sacramentis,* III, n. 652; Wouters, *op. cit.,* p. 15.

[54] *Epitome,* II, n. 397.

[55] S. C. S. O., 19 August, 1891—*Coll. S. C. P. F.,* n. 1765.

[56] Canon 1094; S. C. P. F., 2 July, 1827—*Coll. P. F.,* n. 794; Cappello, III, *De Sacramentis,* n. 655; Wouters, *De Forma . . . Celebrationis Matrimonii,* p. 16.

[57] Vlaming, *Praelectiones Iuris Matrimonialis,* II, n. 191, note 3; Wouters, *loc. cit.;* Cappello, *op. cit.,* n. 655.

[58] S. R. R., 10 February, 1917—*A. A. S.,* IX (1917), 504.

fectively expressed in equivalent signs.[59] The common witnesses, therefore, may assist validly by perceiving consent which is expressed in signs, nods, or which may be inferred from the actions of the bride and bridegroom before, during, and after the ceremony.[60] One who is both blind and deaf could not be a witness to a marriage. If a blind person were certain of the voices, however, he probably could validly act as a witness. Likewise a deaf person, if he were certain of the signs, and knew the persons, and saw them. However, there is no need of adding that persons with such natural defects should not be taken as common witnesses.[61]

As a general rule the parties to the marriage are to choose their own witnesses. This, moreover, is the general practice and witnesses are usually well chosen in advance. The parties to the marriage frequently select the witnesses for the marriage from their intimate friends. Hence in practice many questions which authors are accustomed to discuss are obviated and without meaning, *e. g.*, whether a marriage would be valid if two passers-by overheard the parties as they exchanged mutual consent.[62] Explicit selection of common witnesses, however, is not required for the validity of the marriage. The Sacred Congregation for the Propagation of the Faith has declared a marriage valid which was contracted before a number of persons who had gathered for the occasion, although no one had been particularly designated to act as witnesses. The proviso of the reply of the Congregation was that the marriage was valid as long as those present were certain of the exchange of consent.[63] An implied designation of witnesses will suffice such as is obtained when the parties knowing of the presence of certain people express their consent before them.[64] If the parties positively exclude common witnesses, it

[59] Canon 1088, § 2.

[60] Payen, *De Matrimonio,* II, n. 1764; Wouters, *op. cit.*, pp. 16, 17.

[61] Gasparri, *De Matrimonio,* 3 ed., n. 1161; in his fourth edition, n. 965, he expresses the contrary view regarding a deaf person: Vlaming, *Praelectiones Iuris Matrimonialis,* II, n. 576; Cronin, *New Matrimonial Legislation,* p. 83; Wouters, *op. cit.*, p. 17.

[62] Gasparri, *De Matrimonio,* 4 ed., n. 964.

[63] S. C. P. F., 2 July, 1824—*Coll. P. F.*, n. 794.

[64] Vlaming, *Praelectiones Iuris Matrimonialis,* II, n. 577; Cappello, *De Sacramentis,* III, n. 653; Gasparri, *De Matrimonio,* 4 ed., n. 963.

is very probable that the marriage will be invalid even though they were overheard.[65] The requirement of the law is that the marriage be contracted *coram testibus,* and that they be able to bear testimony to it. This, the witnesses can do, whether they have been implicitly or explicitly chosen. The pastor should see that there are two witnesses besides himself and the parties; that they accompany the bride and bridegroom to the altar, and are attentive during the ceremony, especially at the moment when the mutual consent to the marriage is manifested.

[65] Gasparri, *loc. cit.*

CHAPTER IV

VALID ASSISTANCE AT MARRIAGE

Canon 1095, § 1. Parochus et loci Ordinarius valide matrimonio assistunt;

1. A die tantummodo adeptae canonicae possessionis beneficii ad norman canons 334, § 3, 1444, § 1, vel initi officii, nisi per sententiam fuerint excommunicati vel interdicti vel suspensi ab officio aut tales declarati;

2. Intra fines dumtaxat sui territorii; in quo matrimoniis nedum suorum subditorum, sed etiam non subditorum valide assistunt;

3. Dummodo neque vi neque metu gravi constricti requirant excipiantque contrahentium consensum.

According to canon 1094, as was explained in the preceding chapter a pastor, and local Ordinary (or a priest delegated by either) receive a general mandate to assist at marriage in the rôle of the official witness of the Church (*testis auctorizabilis*). The fact, however, that one is a pastor or local Ordinary does not empower him to assist at marriages anywhere, or in whatever manner he pleases. In canon 1095 § 1 the Code of Canon Law lays down conditions which carefully determine when a priest validly assists at a marriage; in canon 1097 it legislates for the lawfulness of this assistance. Hence two important phases of assistance at marriage stand out, namely, validity and liceity. In the present chapter only the conditions requisite for *valid assistance* will be considered. The Code lays down conditions for the validity of assistance at marriage which (a) govern the time limit of competence (beginning, duration, and cessation), (b) the extent of competence to assist, (c) the manner of assisting at marriage. In separate articles these conditions will be examined in detail. Since each condition is required for validity the absence of only one will suffice to invalidate the marriage.

Article I. Time of Competence

1. *Canonical Possession of Benefice*

Before a priest who has been appointed to a parish or nominated to a See may validly assist at marriage he must take canonical possession of his benefice. A careful distinction is made between *nomination* or *appointment* to a benefice and *canonical possession* of the same. The method of taking possession of a benefice for a residential Bishop is described in canon 334, § 3. He takes possession personally or through a proxy by showing the Apostolic Letters to the cathedral chapter in the presence of the secretary of the chapter, or of the chancellor, who records the fact in the Chancery. The act of taking juridical possession of a See is performed in the chapter. In the United States there are no cathedral chapters and their place is taken by the diocesan consultors (canon 427). Accordingly, the consultors must meet to hear or inspect the papal document. The chancellor of the diocese must be present in order to make a record of the proceedings.[1]

For the canonical possession of a benefice such as a parish the common law does not prescribe any definite procedure. Canon 1444, § 1, states that the method of taking canonical possession of a parish will be determined by diocesan statute or legitimate custom. It adds that the Ordinary may dispense (in writing, however) from the formalities in practice and in this case the dispensation takes the place of formal installation. The ceremony of installation will be of such a nature as to signify that the priest is now the pastor and will illustrate in a characteristic manner his duties and responsibilities, as for example, conducting him to the church, handing him the key to the tabernacle, etc.[2] In the United States the episcopal letter usually indicates the day when the appointment to a pastorate is to

[1] Augustine, *Commentary on Canon Law,* II, p. 350.

[2] Formal installation of the new pastor is observed in a few dioceses in this country. The following is an account of the ceremony observed in the Diocese of Peoria, Illinois, as contained in a communication from the Chancellor of Peoria: "The Dean will lead the new Pastor into the church, where a short Adoration will be made before the Blessed Sacrament, the Dean and the Pastor kneeling on the lowest step before the Altar. Thereupon, the Dean, seated

be effective and the general understanding is that the newly appointed pastor takes possession of the parish when he informally comes to the parish residence with the intention of assuming his duties.[3] Coady points out that this practice is not in conformity with the Code which calls for an installation of the pastor. The Ordinary, he remarks, may dispense from the procedure in individual instances but he feels that he cannot do away with it altogether. Moreover, he says that the very giving of a dispensation indicates that some form of installation is supposed, otherwise there would be nothing from which to dispense. While Coady admits that in the absence of the prescribed form of corporal institution of the priest as pastor, the appointee, following the instructions of the Ordinary, probably legitimately takes possession of the parish, he urges that some form of installation be adopted in all dioceses.[4]

The competence of a pastor and local Ordinary must be reckoned exactly from the moment they take possession of their benefice. A marriage performed even one half hour before the moment of possession will be invalid.[5]

2. *Entrance Into Office*

In the preceding chapter (chapter III) it was seen that certain ecclesiastics have power to assist at marriage, but do not possess any

before the Altar in the Epistle corner, will receive from the new Pastor, kneeling before him, the Profession of Faith and the prescribed oath. Thereupon the Dean will hand the keys of the church to the new Pastor as a symbol of the Pastor's appointment and then he will hand him the Key of the Tabernacle signifying that the Pastor is the custodian of the Blessed Sacrament. Thereupon the Dean will lead the new Pastor to the Confessional, indicating thereby that it is the new Pastor's special duty to hear confessions and reconcile sinners to God. The Dean may make a short address presenting the Pastor to the congregation and the Pastor may address a few words to his people. If the Installation takes place in the afternoon or evening, and there is a sufficient number of people present, the ceremony may conclude with Benediction of the Blessed Sacrament." *Cf.*, also Rossi, *De Paroecia*, n. 181; Coady, *Appointment of Pastors*, pp. 127 ss.

[3] Lydon, *Marriage Legislation in the New Code*, p. 243.

[4] *Appointment of Pastors*, pp. 127-130.

[5] Gasparri, *De Matrimonio*, 4 ed., n. 970; Rossi, *De Matrimonii Celebratione*, p. 74.

benefice, *e. g.*, Vicar General, or Vicar Capitular. It is to them that the words, *initi officii* of canon 1095, § 1, n. 1, refer. They assist validly at marriage from the moment they enter on their office. Usually the time will be mentioned in the official document of appointment.[6]

The competence to witness marriages is enjoyed by pastor and local Ordinary as long as they retain their benefice. The same is to be said of ecclesiastics who assist at marriage in virtue of an office; their right to witness marriages lasts for the time that they are in office. Authorization to witness marriage is lost by express and explicit resignation under the conditions described in canons 184-187. It is likewise lost by tacit resignation which occurs in the circumstances mentioned in canon 188.[7] In the event of a transfer a former benefice is vacated when the new one is legitimately occupied, unless otherwise determined by law or the will of a superior (canon 194, § 1). Assistance rendered by a pastor who had lost his benefice, but unknown to his people, might be valid because of common error. Likewise, assistance which is rendered when the pastor is in positive and probable doubt about his authority to witness marriage would be valid (canon 209).[8]

A pastor or local Ordinary cannot assist validly at marriage if he has been excommunicated, suspended from office, or placed under interdict by a declaratory or condemnatory sentence, or decree. A declaratory sentence states that a penalty *latae sententiae* has been incurred. It may be issued by a judge or legitimate superior when the guilt of the party has been established (canon 2223, § 4). A condemnatory sentence is understood in reference to a penalty *ferendae sententiae*. When the guilt of a person concerning a certain crime punishable by law has been established, a judge or legitimate superior may be obliged, or it may be left to his discretion to inflict the punishment decreed (canon 2223, §§ 2, 3).[9] Hence, if the pastor

[6] Cappello, *De Sacramentis*, III, 661, n. 6; De Smet, *Bethrothment and Marriage*, 1, n. 109.

[7] Augustine, *Commentary on Canon Law*, II, pp. 159-161.

[8] Gasparri, *De Matrimonio*, 4 ed., n. 969; Rossi, *De Celebratione Matrimonii*, p. 75.

[9] Rossi, *De Matrimonii Celebratione*, p. 82 in note.

were to incur an excommunication, or some other penalty *latae sententiae* which according to canon 1095, § 1, n. 1, deprives him of his qualification to witness marriages, he could validly assist until a declaratory sentence was passed upon him. Likewise, were he to commit a crime punishable by law with penalties which disqualify him as an official witness of the Church for marriage, he could assist validly until the penalty was inflicted by a condemnatory sentence. One, however, who lays violent hands upon the person of the Holy Father is *ipso facto vitandus* (canon 2343, § 1, n. 1), and according to the law the customary conditions for declaring one *vitandus* (canon 2258) need not be observed.[10] If a pastor or Ordinary, therefore, were guilty of this crime, his competence to witness marriages would cease immediately.

It may be asked whether a pastor can licitly assist at a marriage before a sentence of excommunication is passed upon him. It would seem that ordinarily he cannot, as assistance at marriage implies the active use of sacramentals which is forbidden to all excommunicates by canon 2261, § 1. However, before a declaratory sentence is passed, one is not obliged to observe a penalty *latae sententiae* if there is danger to his good reputation in doing so (canon 2232).[11]

Under the decree *Tametsi* a pastor could assist at marriage even though he was excommunicated or suspended.[12] Under the decree *Ne Temere* a pastor was not disqualified unless he had been suspended from office, or excommunicated by name and by public decree.[13] The Code does not require that the penalty be known publicly. In the event, therefore, that it remains unknown and is secret (which will occur infrequently with regard to a declaratory or condemnatory sentence or decree) the pastor could validly witness a marriage on the strength of supplied jurisdiction in common error.[14]

The general opinion is that excommunication, suspension from office, and personal interdict, are the only penalties which deprive

[10] Cappello, *De Censuris*, n. 141.

[11] Hyland, *Excommunication*, p. 104.

[12] Benedict XIV, *De Synodo Dioecesana*, lib. XII, c. 5, n. 2.

[13] S. C. C., decret., *Ne Temere*, 2 August, 1907, Art. IV, 1—*Fontes*, n. 4340.

[14] Chelodi, *Ius Matrimoniale*, n. 132, note 5; Gasparri, *De Matrimonio*, 4 ed., n. 969.

the official witness of competence to assist at marriage. Canon 1095, § 1, n. 1, names these penalties and no others. The disjunctive wording of the canon, " . . . nisi per sententiam fuerint excommunicati, *vel* interdicti, *vel* suspensi ab officio . . . " seems to strengthen the belief that the punishments which disqualify the pastor and others to witness marriage are listed taxatively.[15] Suspension from jurisdiction, therefore, or from orders, or *a divinis,* or from a benefice will not necessarily deprive one of his competence to assist at marriage. Gasparri mentions that a priest under any of these penalties may also lawfully assist at a marriage if there be no danger of scandal.[16] The view therefore of those canonists who would disqualify a priest from assisting if he had been deprived of jurisdiction by sentence seems to go beyond the limits of canon 1095, § 1, n. 1. Penal laws are subject to strict interpretation (canon 19). Moreover, the act of assisting at marriage, since it is not one of jurisdiction, may be discharged by one who has been deprived of jurisdiction.

It is to be noted that a general suspension, that is, one without further qualification, includes suspension from office (canon 2278, § 2). Hence a pastor who has been simply suspended either by a declaratory or condemnatory sentence or decree is disqualified from acting as official witness of the Church at marriage.

Article II. Limits of Competence

The preceding article considered when competence to assist at marriage began and when it was suspended or ceased. For those who are given authority to assist at marriage by the general authorization of canon 1094, it is important to know where this mandate is to be exercised, and over whom. When the decree *Tametsi* was the law of the Church (1564-1908) this question could be answered easily by the *parochus proprius.* He could assist at the marriage of his subjects everywhere. For others (non-subjects) he needed the delegation of their proper pastor. This practice lead to serious difficulties and often gave rise to doubts about the validity of marriages as so much depended on the *parochus proprius,*—for he alone could validly

[15] Gasparri, *op. cit.*, n. 973; Wouters, *De Forma . . Celebrationis Matrimonii,* p. 18.

[16] Gasparri, *loc. cit.*

assist or delegate. It was often very difficult and sometimes almost impossible to know with certainty who was one's proper pastor. The new legislation of the decree *Ne Temere* adopted the principle common in civil law that a notary was competent for a definite territory, and it established as the basis of valid assistance for marriage the limits of the parish or diocese. The Code renewed the law as expressed in the decree *Ne Temere.* Today, therefore, within the boundaries of his diocese an Ordinary assists *validly* at the marriages of his subjects and at the marriages of *non subjects* as well. Outside his diocese, he had no authority to assist at marriage. To assist at the marriage of a subject in another diocese he would need proper delegation. The same is to be said for the pastor. Within parochial limits he validly assists at *all marriages* whether of parishioners or non-parishioners; outside his parish he is not competent. Likewise, with all others who have a general mandate to assist at marriage in virtue of canon 1094.[17] It can be only exercised within the limits of their proper territory. The territorial limits must be strictly observed. Even crossing the street into another diocese or parish would invalidate the marriage performed there without express delegation.[18] In thus placing on a territorial basis the pastor's competence the decree *Ne Temere* and the Code removed a great source of trouble and at the same time afford greater opportunity to the parties to unite themselves validly in marriage.[19]

The pastor however cannot assist *lawfully* at marriages of non-subjects but must carefully observe the provisions of canon 1097, which legislates for lawful assistance at marriage. He may assist at marriages in his own church or in any other church in his parish. The church of a religious exempt community is to be considered as part of the territory of the parish or diocese in which it is located, and the local pastor and Ordinary may assist validly at marriages in it.[20] For

[17] These are enumerated in Chapter III, Articles I and II.

[18] Gasparri, *De Matrimonio,* 4 ed., n. 975; Ayrinhac-Lydon, *Marriage Legislation in the Code of Canon Law,* p. 244; Rossi, *De Celebratione Matrimonii,* p. 76; Leitner, *Katholisches Eherecht,* p. 195.

[19] Bory, *Un Commento concernente la celebrazione del Matrimonio Cattolico,* p. 25.

[20] S. C. de Sacramentis, *Romana et aliarum,* 13 March, 1910, ad VIII—*Fontes,* n. 2101.

licit assistance the permission of the Superior of the community will have to be obtained.[21]

Hospital chaplains or chaplains of orphanages, homes for the aged, sanatoria, universities and the like, who have *full parochial power* can assist at the marriage of the persons who are subject to their authority, but only in the locality wherein they exercise jurisdiction.[22] If the chaplains in question do not enjoy full parochial authority, they will have to receive delegation for each marriage from the pastor within whose parish the hospital, home, orphanage or university is located. They may, however, be appointed as *vicarii cooperatores* of the pastor and thereby become capable of receiving general delegation for marriage.

Concerning the right of a personal pastor to assist at marriage it will be necessary to distinguish between one who is a personal pastor in the strict sense of the term, and others who come within a wider use of the title "personal pastor." Personal pastor in the strict use of the word is a priest who exercises jurisdiction over certain persons in virtue of some quality that they possess, *e. g.*, in as much as they are members of a royal family; or belong to a special religious rite; or to a particular class of men, *e. g.*, soldiers.[23] It is characteristic of a purely personal pastor that he is bound to his subject by ties other than that of territory. He follows them wherever they go and assists validly and lawfully at their marriages wherever they may be,—*but only at their marriages.* He has no competence in the marriages of non-subjects.[24] The subjects of strictly personal pastors, however, may be validly married by the pastor of the parish within which they are dwelling or by any other

[21] Wouters, *De Forma . . . Celebrationis Matrimonii,* p. 18.

[22] X. Num cappellani seu rectores piorum cuiusvis generis locorum, a parochiali jurisdictione exemptorum adsistere valide possint absque parochi vel Ordinarii delegatione?

Ad X. "Affirmative pro personis sibi creditis in loco tamen ubi jurisdictionem exercent, dummodo constet ipsis commissam fuisse plenam potestatem parochialem"—S. C. C., *Romana et aliarum,* February, 1908—*A. S. S.*, XLI (1908), 108-111.

[23] Gasparri, *De Matrimonio,* 4 ed., n. 976; Wernz-Vidal, *Jus Canonicum,* V, n. 535; Cappello, *De Sacramentis,* III, n. 668.

[24] S. C. C., *Romana et aliarum,* 1 February, 1908, ad VII—*Fontes,* n. 4344.

pastor within the confines of his parish. The reason is because canon 1095, § 1, n. 2, explicitly declares that a pastor assist validly at the marriages of non-subjects within his territory.[25] The Sacred Congregation of the Sacraments declared that personal pastors in India, *attentis peculiaribus circumstantiis,* retained exclusive jurisdiction over their subjects.

Personal pastors in a broader sense are priests who have the care of persons speaking a certain language or belonging to a certain nationality or race but whose charge over these people is limited to a definite territory (a village, city, or diocese). Their authority may be restricted exclusively to the persons subjected to them; that is to say, they may have personal jurisdiction to be exercised over these people within a determined territory but that they do not possess a territorial parish. On the other hand, a personal pastor may have *territorial* as well as *personal* jurisdiction for canon 216, § 4, indicates that national parishes may be lawfully established in a diocese. Doubtlessly they are exceptions to the rule of canon 216, § 1, but they are frequently needed. Hence, at times a personal pastor may be found having jurisdiction with other pastors in a given territory.[26] If the personal pastor has no territorial but only personal jurisdiction, he validly assists at the marriage of subjects only,—or marriages in which at least one party is under his care,—and in that territory only.[27] On the other hand, if the personal pastor has territorial as well as personal jurisdiction, he validly and lawfully assists at the marriages of his own people and can also validly witness marriages of non-subjects.[28] Whether or not the personal pastors have terri-

[25] Gasparri, *De Matrimonio,* 4 ed., n. 976; Wernz-Vidal, *Jus Canonicum,* V, n. 535; Cappello, *De Sacramentis,* III, n. 669; Vlaming, *Praelectiones Juris Matrimonialis,* II, 536; Vermeersch-Creusen, *Epitome,* II, n. 393.

[26] Gasparri, *De Matrimonio,* 4 ed., n. 976; Cappello, *De Sacramentis,* III, n. 668; Wernz-Vidal, *Jus Canonicum,* V, n. 535; Creagh, *Commentary in Ne Temere,* p. 32.

[27] IX. Ubinam et quomodo parochus, qui in territorio aliis parochis assignato nonnullas personas vel familias sibi subditos habet matrimoniis adsistere valeat?

Ad IX. "Affirmative, quoad suos subditos tantum ubique in dicto territorio, facto verbo cum Ssmo"—S. C. C., *Romana et aliarum,* 1 February 1908—*Fontes,* n. 4344.

[28] VIII. Ubinam et quomodo parochi qui territorium exclusive proprium non

torial as well as personal jurisdiction is a question of fact. National pastors in this country are considered by some writers as purely personal pastors,[29] and hence validly assist only at the marriage of the people under their charge. Others believe that these pastors have territorial limits sufficient to fulfill the requirements of canon 216, § 1, and are, therefore, pastors of territorial parishes. Accordingly the pastors of national parishes validly and lawfully assist at the marriage of their subjects within their parish limits; likewise, within said limits they assist validly at the marriages of non-subjects but *unlawfully* unless some title to lawful assistance according to canon 1097 can be invoked.[30] The question, as has been mentioned, is one of fact: what was the original intention and purpose in mind when the national parish was established? As far as the validity of marriage performed by national pastors of persons who are not their subjects there need be no doubt, for "if the power of the national pastor is theoretically doubtful, in practice the marriages witnessed are valid in virtue of canon 209, either because of common error on the part of the people, who certainly judge that any pastor in the district can validly witness weddings, or on the other principle of probable or positive doubt." [31]

According to canon 451, § 3, the authority of military chaplains is to be learned from special concessions of the Holy See. Hence little can be said in the way of a definite rule. The conditions in each country must be examined.[32] In some countries such as France and Belgium military chaplains are under the supervision of the local Ordinary and receive their authority from him.[33] In some countries

habentes, territorium cum alio vel cum aliis parochis retinent, matrimoniis adsistere valeant?

Ad VIII. "Affirmative in territorio cumulativo habito"—S. C. C., *Romana et aliarum,* 1 February, 1908—*Fontes,* n. 4344.

[29] L. Raymond, *Competentia Matrimonialis Parochi Gentilicii, seu Personalis —Periodica,* XVI (1927), 257*-263*.

[30] *National Pastors and Assistance at Marriage*—A. E. R., LXXX (1929), 88-94.

[31] Ayrinhac-Lydon, *Matrimonial Legislation in the Code of Canon Law,* p. 245.

[32] Prümmer, *Manuale Theologiae Moralis,* 111, n. 758.

[33] Vermeersch-Creusen, *Epitome,* I, n. 492.

the Holy See has erected a *dioecesis castrensis* over which an Ordinary presides, usually entitled *Ordinarius* or *Episcopus Castrensis.* All regular military chaplains within his diocese are directly subject to him and receive from him a pagella containing the faculties which he grants in virtue of authority from the Holy See. An *Episcopus Castrensis* was appointed by the Holy See for the United States and her possessions on November 24, 1917, in the person of the present Cardinal Archbishop of New York.[34] According to the faculties issued to Army and Navy Chaplains of the United States of America, chaplains validly assist at a marriage provided that at least one of the parties is a subject of the military diocese. They may marry their subjects anywhere, but if the marriage is to be celebrated outside a military post, camp, reservation, or any other place which can be said to belong to the United States Military Service, the permission of the local pastor, or the Ordinary of the place is to be obtained for the lawful celebration of the marriage.[35] The following are indicated in the Faculties as subjects of the military diocese; (1) all who are actively engaged in military service of the United States of America; (2) employes of the American Government provided they live on the military post, camp, reservation, or other place which can be said to pertain to the United States Military Service; (3) the families and relatives who are immediately dependent upon the foregoing; (4) members of the State Militia for the time they are under the military authority of the American Government.[36]

Article III. Manner of Assistance

The condition laid down in canon 1095, § 1, n. 3, governs the manner in which the official witness of the Church is to assist at a

[34] This information was received from the present Vicar-General Castrensis, Monsignor George J. Waring, in a letter dated January 18, 1934.

[35] "Assistendi matrimoniis quae invalida erunt nisi alterutra pars sit sub ditus *Diocesis Castrensis.* Praeterea omniis Cappellanus districte vetatur assistere cuipiam matrimonio etiam duorum subditorum *Diocesis Castrensis,* extra fines praesidii, castrorum, stationis vel cuiusvis loci ad servitium militare Gubernii Americani pertinentis, nisi prius obtenta licentia parochi vel Ordinaii loci in cuius territorio matrimonium contrahitur"—Faculties issued to military chaplains by *Episcopus Castrensis* of U. S. A., n. VI.

[36] *Ibid., Normae Speciales Dioecesis Castrensis,* Par. 1.

marriage. He must ask the parties who present themselves to him if they take each other for man and wife; and he must do so, unconstrained by any force or grave fear. A brief historical review of the former discipline concerning the manner in which the priest acted at marriage will explain why the condition spoken of in this article is so strongly stressed.

During the time when the decree *Tametsi* was the law of the Church, despite the directions of the Council of Trent as to manner of assisting at marriage, and the rubrics of the Ritual that the priest should ask and receive the consent of the parties, flagrant examples of violation of these precepts occurred. In the year 1581 the Bishop of Jaen in Spain proposed a series of questions to the Sacred Congregation of the Council several of which concerned the manner of assisting of the pastor at marriage.[37] From the replies given it will be seen that under the decree *Tametsi* in assisting at marriage the priest had to know what was being done (ad IV). A marriage was valid at which he was present although against his will and under compulsion (ad III), and it was not necessary for the validity of the marriage that he should be invited or requested to act or that he should take any active and authoritative part in the ceremony (ad V). This understanding of the legislation gave rise to the so-called "surprise marriage" which took place when persons wishing to contract marriage and being confronted by some opposition would come upon the pastor

[37] "III. Si invitus, et compulsus per vim adsit Sacerdos, dum contrahitur matrimonium, praecedente vel non praecedente, dicta prohibitione, utrum tale matrimonium subsistat?—Resp.—Subsistere.

"IV. Si Sacerdos adfuerit, nihil tamen eorum quae agebantur, vidit, neque audivit, utrum tale matrimonium valide contrahatur, vel potius, tamquam sine Sacerdote nullius sit ponderis et momenti?—Resp. Non valere, si Sacerdos non intellexit; nisi tamen affectasset non intellegere.

"V. Si adsit Sacerdos, dum contrahitur matrimonium, casu non cogitans se esse ad id vocatum; sed aliud agens, audit duos inter se contrahentes matrimonium, utrum sit validum tale matrimonium, in quo fuit praesens, non tamen certioratus, nec ad id expresse vocatus, neque interponens suam auctoritatem dicto vel facto; vel potius sit nullum, quasi assistentia auctoritativa per Concilium requiratur et non nuda vel casualis praesentia? Resp. Valere, etiamsi Parochus aliam ob causam adhibitus sit ad illum actum." Benedict XIV, *De Synodo Dioecesana,* lib. XIII, c. 23, n. 1.

unawares and declare themselves man and wife.[38] These marriages were an offence to the reverence and dignity due to the Sacrament as well as an insult to the priest, the official witness of the Church. It was strongly desired that something should be done to remedy the situation. Accordingly when the Sacred Congregation of the Council gave thought to a modification of the decree *Tametsi* it directed the consultors who were appointed to draft the changes that they incorporate into the new decree a provision which would require under pain of nullity that the pastor be invited and requested to act and that he do so freely.[39] This request was observed to the letter[40] Later the Congregation interpreted the meaning of the words, "invited and requested," declaring that implicit invitation or request would suffice.[41] The legislation of the Code is the same as that contained in the decree *Ne Temere,* with the exception that the Code has omitted the words *invitati vel rogati* (canon 1095, § 1, n. 3). It requires that the priest under penalty of invalidity assist free from force or fear, and that he ask and receive the consent of the parties.

1. *Freedom From Force or Fear*

The official witness must assist unconstrained by force or grave fear, *e. g.*, fear of serious harm, or of some dire happening. The fear must influence the priest until the marriage is celebrated and cause him to assist at the marriage. If the pastor is brought to the church unwillingly and under constraint but upon arriving there changes his mind and willingly and of his own accord witnesses the marriage, the assistance thus rendered will be valid.[42] The canon indicates that the fear spoken of is *metus ab extrinseco,* since it speaks of the pastor being constrained to assist. This can only mean extrinsic fear.[43] The

[38] Pallottini, *Collectio S. C. Concilii,* XIII, p. 281.

[39] *A. S. S.,* XL (1907), 521.

[40] S. C. C., decr., *Ne Temere,* 2 August, 1907, Art. IV—*Fontes,* n. 4340.

[41] S. C. de Sacramentis, *Romana et aliarum,* 28 March, 1908, ad IV—*Fontes,* n. 4349.

[42] Wouters, *De Forma . . . Celebrationis Matrimonii,* p. 19; Gasparri, *De Matrimonio,* 4 ed., n. 979.

[43] Vlaming, *Praelectiones Iuris Matrimonialis,* II, n. 577; Payen, *De Matrimonio,* II, n. 1774.

fear must have been caused either directly or indirectly in order to make the pastor assist at the marriage. To understand fear inflicted for other reasons as invalidating marriage would give rise to innumerable anxieties about marriages contracted.[44] Fear must not be readily supposed, but must be established by a careful scrutiny of the circumstances of the case.[45]

The Code requires that the fear be grave but says nothing about the reason which causes it. Does it mean that only grave fear which is *unjustly* inflicted invalidates the assistance; or will grave fear which is *justly* caused have the same effect? An example of just fear would be a punishment threatened by the Ordinary when a priest unjustly refuses to assist at a marriage or a threat made by the parties to report a priest who *unjustly* refuses to assist at their marriage. Gasparri says that fear of this type will not invalidate assistance.[46] Wouters is unwilling to admit a general statement to the effect that the fear spoken of in the canon must be unjustly inflicted. His reason is that the Code does not distinguish. The just fear mentioned in the examples above will not invalidate the assistance according to him, however, because it is ordained, and intended for the observance of the law itself.[47] Vidal holds that no distinction was made by the Code because it is quite impossible to conceive of fear which would be justly inflicted by the parties and at the same time be grave. He considers the question of no practical value.[48]

For practical purposes it is well to note that fraud on the part of the parties to obtain the assistance of the pastor, while sinful, does not affect the validity of the marriage for the Code does not mention it as having an invalidating effect. Hence if the parties should de-

[44] Wouters, *De Forma . . . Celebrationis Matrimonii*, p. 19; Payen, *loc cit.;* Cerato, *De Matrimonio*, n. 92. 4.

[45] Wouters, *loc cit.;* Cerato, *loc. cit.*

[46] Gasparri, *De Matrimonio*, 4 ed., n. 979.

[47] Wouters, *De Forma . . . Celebrationis Matrimonii*, p. 19.

[48] Wernz-Vidal, *Jus Canonicum*, V, n. 537, note 26; Ayrinhac-Lydon, *Marriage Legislation in the New Code of Canon Law*, p. 244; Vlaming, *Praelectiones Juris Matrimonialis*, II, 577; De Becker, *De Matrimonio* (ed. nova), p. 137; Payen, *De Matrimonio*, II, 1774; Chelodi, *Ius Matrimoniale*, n. 133.

ceive the pastor about their residence, or even their names, the assistance rendered would be valid.[49]

2. *Interrogation of the Parties*

The priest must not only be free from any force or influence of fear when he assists at a marriage but he must also interrogate the parties as to their desire to marry and receive from them a mutual expression of their consent (canon 1095, § 1, n. 3). This is not to be understood as an invitation tendered by the priest to marriage but an inquiry into the minds of the parties.[50] The Ritual contains the formula which is to be used at the marriage ceremony.[51] It is to be noted that the words of the Ritual are not necessary for the validity of marriage.[52] The Code wishes the priest to take an active part in the ceremony by asking for the consent of the parties and receiving it when expressed. This requirement does away with the so-called "surprise marriages." The priest may put the question by means of signs, or even in writing, if circumstances are such that he cannot ask it in words. Correspondingly, the spouses may answer with signs, or writing in case of necessity. Provided the priest manifests his interrogation with sufficient clearness and the parties sufficiently externalize or manifest to him their consent to marriage the requirements of the Code will be fulfilled.[53] Accordingly a blind priest or a deaf priest might be able to make the necessary investigation and receive the consent of the parties but there would be grave danger attached in such circumstances. A priest who is both deaf and blind cannot assist validly.[54]

[49] Gasparri, *De Matrimonio,* 4 ed., n. 979; Wouters, *De Forma . . . Celebrationis Matrimonii,* p. 19; Payen, *De Matrimonio,* II, n. 1774; Farrugia, *De Matrimonio,* p. 376; Chelodi, *Ius Matrimoniale,* n. 132.

[50] Cappello, *De Sacramentis,* III, n. 671.

[51] Rituale Rom., tit. VII, c. 2. *Ritus celebrandi matrimonii sacramentum,* n. 1, 2.

[52] Vermeersch-Creusen, *Epitome,* II, n. 394.

[53] Wouters, *De Forma . . . Celebrationis Matrimonii,* p. 20; Farrugia, *De Matrimonio,* p. 376; Payen, *De Matrimonio,* II, n. 1774; Cappello, *De Sacramentis,* III, n. 671; Rossi, *De Celebratione Matrimonii,* p. 81.

[54] Rossi, *op. cit.,* p. 81.

The provisions of this canon must be observed even in mixed marriages.[55] Under the decree *Ne Temere* the Holy See tolerated merely passive assistance at marriages contracted between Catholics and non-Catholics in which the non-Catholic refused to make the usual promises. Merely passive assistance implied that the priest was present at the marriage but did not interrogate the parties and receive their mutual consent.[56] Passive assistance was tolerated in Hungary, Bavaria, and parts of Austria in virtue of a special concession of the Holy See[57] With the publication of the Code containing the prescriptions of canon 1095, § 1, n. 3, and canon 1102, § 1, and in conformance with an answer given by the Holy Office to the Bishop of Prague [58] it was generally admitted that mere passive assistance was not permitted in the countries mentioned. The Pontifical Commission for the Interpretation of the Code stated that canon 1102, § 1, abolished any indult permitting passive assistance granted by the Holy See.[59]

[55] Canon 1102, § 1. "In matrimoniis inter partem catholicam et partem acatholicam interrogationes de consensu fieri debent secundum praescriptum canonis 1095, § 1, n. 3."

[56] Aertnys-Damen, *Theologia Moralis,* II, n. 706; *Jus Pontificium.* X (1930), 110-119.

[57] S. C. S. Off., 21 June, 1912—*A. A. S.,* IV (1912), 316; S. C. S. Off., 5 August, 1916—*A. A. S.,* VIII (1916), 443.

[58] S. C. S. Off., 26 November, 1919—*Cfr. Linz. Quart.,* LXXIV (1921), p. 249.

[59] 10 March, 1928—*A. A. S.,* XX (1918), 120.

CHAPTER V

DELEGATION TO ASSIST AT MARRIAGE

Canon 1095, § 2. Parochus et loci Ordinarius qui matrimonio possunt valide assistere, possunt quoque alii sacerdoti licentiam dare ut intra fines sui territorii matrimonio valide assistat.

Canon 1096, § 1. Licentiam assistendi matrimonio concessa ad normam 1095, § 2, dari expresse debet sacerdoti determinato ad matrimonium determinatum, exclusis quibuslibet delegationibus generalibus, nisi agatur de vicariis cooperatoribus pro paroecia cui addicti sunt; secus irrita est.

§ 2. Parochus vel loci Ordinarius licentiam ne concedat, nisi expletis omnibus quae ius constituit pro libertate status comprobanda.

THE pastor and local Ordinary, who can validly assist at a marriage, are empowered by canon 1095, § 2, to give permission to another priest to assist at that marriage within the limits of their territory. The priest thus designated is said to be delegated for the marriage. Canon 1095, § 2, therefore, contains a concession of the legislator to the official witnesses of the Church, whereby they may substitute another priest to act in their official capacity. Such is the concept of delegation for marriage; it is one of substitution, priest N——— acting in the capacity of the *testis auctorizabilis*.[1] The Code is not constant in describing this act of substitution; at times it refers to it as "permission to assist" (canons 1095, § 2; 1096, § 1

[1] Wouters, *De Forma . . . Celebrationis Matrimonii*, p. 21; Rossi, *De Matrimonii Celebratione*, p. 97; Cronin, *New Matrimonial Legislation*, p. 69; Gasparri, *De Matrimonio*, 4 ed., 945; Vlaming, *Praelectiones Juris Matrimonialis*, II, 571; Payen, *De Matrimonio*, II, n. 1776.

and § 2). Again it associates it with delegation, excluding the grant of general delegation for marriages except to assistants (canon 1096, § 1) and referring to the priest who is designated by the pastor as "*sacerdos delegatus*" (canon 1094). The pastor and local Ordinary are not free to delegate whomever they desire, or in whatever manner they please. Canon 1096 carefully prescribes the conditions for valid and lawful delegation. This chapter consists of three articles; the first, treating of the persons who may delegate; the second, considering the manner of delegating; the third discussing the use and cessation of delegation.

Article I. The Active Subject of Delegation

The Code in canon 1095, § 2, lists the pastor and the local Ordinary as the ones who may delegate another priest to assist at marriage. Since December 28, 1927, it is certain that assistants (*vicarii cooperatores*) who have been generally delegated for marriages in their parish may subdelegate.[2] Missionaries who are assigned to territories not as yet divided into quasi-parishes, provided they have received general delegation from their Vicar or Prefect Apostolic, may likewise subdelegate a definite priest for a definite marriage. This follows logically from the Instruction of the Sacred Congregation for the Propagation of the Faith, which declared that missionaries in the circumstances described therein were to be considered assistants of the Vicar or Prefect Apostolic and could be given general delegation for marriages within the Vicariate or Prefecture.[3] It should be carefully noted that the pastor and Ordinary may give general delegation to assistants for the parish to which the assistants are assigned; assistants, however, may subdelegate only for a determined marriage. Likewise, missionaries with general delegation can subdelegate only for a determined marriage. This follows from the analogy which exists between them and assistants.[4] Previous to the decision of the Pontifical Commission, the right of as-

[2] Pontif. Comm. Inter. Cod., 28 December, 1927—*A. A. S.*, XX (1928), 61.

[3] *A. A. S.*, XII (1920), 331, 332

[4] Canon 1096, § 1, compared with the reply of the Pontifical Commission, 27 December, 1927—*A. A. S.*, XX (1928), 61.

sistants to subdelegate was called into question. Canonists of eminence disagreed; the chief argument against the right of subdelegation was that the principle of canon 199, § 3,[5] could not be applied to delegation for marriage, because assistance at marriage is not an act of jurisdiction but a *nudum ministerium.* The decision of the Pontifical Commission ended the controversy and it is now certain that assistants who have *general delegation* for marriage may subdelegate a determined priest for a determined marriage. The assistant cannot give his subdelegate the power to subdelegate again for a special case unless this faculty were granted to him by the one with ordinary power (*e. g.*, the local Ordinary or pastor), in words such as: "You have power at any time to allow your subdelegate to subdelegate for a special case." [6] The Pontifical Commission for the Interpretation of the Code has declared that a pastor and local Ordinary may delegate a priest for a determined marriage and may give him the right to subdelegate another priest for the same marriage.[7] This does not mean that the subdelegated priest has to be known to the pastor or local Ordinary. If this were true, there would not be a case of subdelegation but the original delegator would rather be said to have delegated two priests for the marriage. The subdelegated priest need not be known to the pastor or Ordinary but he must be expressly subdelegated by the delegate and can only assist at the marriage for which delegation had been given.[8]

May the pastor or local Ordinary grant general delegation to an assistant, and at the same time prohibit the assistant from subdelegating? Some authors believe that in virtue of the reply given by the Commission, the right of subdelegation cannot be forbidden, for according to canon 199, § 3, general delegation carries with it the right to subdelegate. They believe that the pastor or local Ordinary is powerless to restrict this provision of the common law. Hence while the pastor and Ordinary are the ones who give general delegation to

[5] "Potestas delegata ad universitatem negotiorum ab eo qui infra Romanum Pontificem habet ordinariam potestatem, potest in singulis casibus subdelegari."

[6] Canon 199, § 5; Ayrinhac-Lydon, *The New Matrimonial Legislation,* p. 250.

[7] 28 December, 1927—*A. A. S.*, XX (1928), 61, 62.

[8] Wernz-Vidal, *Ius Canonicum,* V, n. 538, p. 632, note 41; *Apollinaris,* I (1928), 104-108.

the assistants, it is the common law in canon 199, § 3, which empowers them to subdelegate.[9] Canon 203, § 1,[10] however, seems to convey the idea that the delegator may limit the commission which he gives to another. If, in the grant of general delegation, no mention is made of limitation of subdelegation, the assistant may certainly subdelegate. Any limitation imposed by the one delegating should be very definite, and clear, and unconditional. The Holy See would have to be consulted concerning a marriage which was performed by a priest who was delegated by an assistant who disregarded the limitation of his authority to subdelegate

For the validity of the delegation given by the pastor, local Ordinary, or assistant, in as far as they personally are concerned (for the present only the requirements *ex parte delegantis* will be considered, in the following article the manner of granting delegation will be discussed), two conditions are necessary: (1) they must be in a position to assist validly at the marriage themselves for which they are delegating another; and (2) the marriage in question must be celebrated within the limits of their jurisdiction. The first condition requires that the provisions of the preceding chapter regarding canonical possession, and maintenance of a benefice, excommunication and the like be observed; the second is evident, in as much as a pastor, local Ordinary, or assistant is powerless to assist at marriage beyond the limits of his jurisdiction. They cannot, therefore, authorize another to perform a task for which they themselves are incapable.[11]

The pastor and local Ordinary are directed by the Code to institute the customary pre-nuptial investigation concerning the freedom of the parties to marry. This is to be done and accomplished before delegation to assist is given to another priest (canon 1096, § 2). This investigation is necessary for the lawful concession of the

9 *Periodica,* XVIII (1929), 94, 95.

10 "Delegatus qui sive circa res sive circa personas mandati sui fines excedit, nihil agit."

11 Reg. 72: "Qui facit per alium est perinde ac si faciat per seipsum"; Reg. 79: "Nemo potest plus iuris transferre in alium, quam sibi competere dignoscatur"—R. J., in VI°.

delegation,—not for its validity.[12] Under the decree *Ne Temere,* the burden of investigation was placed on the priest who had been delegated.[13] It is more within the province of the pastor to establish the freedom of the parties to marry and in this matter the pastor is usually more suited than the priest who is delegated for the marriage. The Code makes no exception to this obligation of the pastor; hence this ruling would seem to hold even when assistants have general delegation. While it is true that the actual work of investigating the freedom of the parties is frequently carried on by the assistants, it should be done under the supervision of the pastor. He in the parish has the *cura animarum* and, especially, the care of marriages. The responsibility, it would seem, rests ultimately with him.

In this article on the active subject of delegation for assistance at marriage, one item remains to be treated,—the extent of the titles, pastor and Ordinary. In Chapter III, the meaning of pastor and local Ordinary was discussed at length. Those who are included in these terms may delegate another priest for marriage under the conditions which have already been described. On the 20th of May, 1923, the Pontifical Commission replied to several doubts which had been proposed concerning the power of delegation possessed by those priests who according to canon 451, § 2, are to be considered the equal of pastors. It declared: (1) an administrator of a vacant parish (canon 472) could delegate for marriage; (2) the vicar substitute (canon 465, § 4), who has been approved by the Ordinary, could delegate unless the Ordinary limited his power; if the substitute is a religious he may delegate once he has received the Ordinary's approval and before the approbation of his superior; (3) *vicarius supplens* (canon 465, § 5), may delegate before he receives the approval of the Ordinary and until the Ordinary notifies him to the contrary; (4) the *vicarius adjutor* (canon 475), may delegate if he supplies the pastor in everything.[14]

[12] Gasparri, *De Matrimonio,* 4 ed., n. 960.

[13] S. C. C., decret., *"Ne Temere,"* 2 August, 1907, Art. VI—*Fontes,* 4340.

[14] Pontif. Comm. Inter. Cod., May 20, 1923—*A. A. S.,* XVI (1924), 114-115.

Article II. How Delegation Is to Be Granted

The Code does not leave the pastor and local Ordinary free to delegate whomever they desire, or in whatever manner they please. Likewise, it does not leave the situation unclarified so that any priest may feel that he can assist at marriage. It lays down, on the contrary, very stringent regulations which direct the granting of delegation, conditions which affect the validity of the delegation, and consequently the validity of the marriage (canon 1096, § 2: . . . *secus* [*delegatio*] *irrita est*). The conditions for valid delegation to a marriage are: (1) it must be given expressly, (2) to a priest, (3) to a definite priest, (4) for a definite marriage. General delegation, *i. e.*, delegation for "any marriage which may arise," cannot be granted, except to assistants (*vicarii cooperatores*), and then only for the parish to which they are assigned. The purpose of the present article is to discuss the four conditions already referred to and to treat other questions having a bearing on the granting of delegation for marriage.

1. *The Delegation Must Be Expressly Granted*

Delegation is expressly given in the following ways: (a) if given in writing; (b) also if given by word of mouth, telephone, or telegraph; (c) by evident signs, such as the nod of the head. The Code is silent on the explanation of the word *expresse*, and the above named ways are accepted by canonists.[15] The granting of delegation in writing is preferable and urged by all so that subsequent doubts may be easily avoided. The Roman Ritual would seem to suppose written permission to assist at marriage but the Code does not mention it.[16] Delegation can be *special* for a particular marriage, or *general* for all marriages which may arise in a certain parish. As has been already mentioned, only assistants can receive general delegation for marriages. The Code does not give any set formula in which delegation is to

[15] Chelodi, *Jus Matrimoniale*, n. 133; Vlaming, *Praelectiones Juris Matrimonialis*, II, n. 574; Wernz-Vidal, *Jus Canonicum*, V, n. 538; Gasparri, *De Matrimonio*, 4 ed., n. 955; Wouters, *De Forma . . . Celebrationis Matrimonii*, p. 24.

[16] *Rit. Romanum*, t. X., c. 5, with canon 1096, § 1.

be granted. This is left to the one who delegates. The all important factor is that it be *expressly* granted and not presumed.

Express delegation, therefore, excludes *presumed* and *tacit* delegation. Presumed delegation is had when a priest who is not delegated for a marriage, assists at it nevertheless, because he believes that the pastor certainly would have delegated him if he knew the circumstances, *e. g.*, while the pastor is away the brother of the bride, a priest, arrives unexpectedly and is anxious to assist at the marriage. The assistant (it is supposed) cannot delegate him. No one is at hand from whom he may receive delegation but he presumes to assist on the strength of the fact that the pastor would have unhesitatingly delegated him for the marriage of his sister. Such delegation is entirely invalid for in truth it is no delegation at all. It is simply *presumed*. It was not recognized under the decree *Tametsi* nor the decree *Ne Temere* nor *a fortiori*, under the law of the Code which requires express delegation.[17] Tacit delegation is had when a pastor, aware of the fact that another priest without any authority is about to assist at a marriage within his parish, does not raise any objection.[18] Before the Code many authors admitted the validity of tacit delegation,[19] but they advised against the use of it.[20] Tacit delegation is certainly invalid today for the Code requires that delegation be expressed.

Vlaming observes that delegation for marriage may sometimes be implied and deduced from the actions of the pastor. He says that the requirement of the Code for *expressed delegation* must not be confused with and understood to mean *explicit delegation*. Accordingly, therefore, if from the actions of the pastor it is evident that the priest in question is to perform the marriage between N.— and N.— but he fails to say to the priest "I delegate you"—in such circumstances Vlaming is inclined to regard the delegation as valid. The example given illustrates the case: pastor A is called away, and cannot per-

[17] Gasparri, *De Matrimonio,* 4 ed., n. 954; Vlaming, *Praelectiones Iuris Matrimonialis,* II, n. 574; Cronin, *The New Matrimonial Legislation,* p. 73.

[18] Gasparri, *De Matrimonio,* 4 ed., n. 954; Ayrinhac-Lydon, *Marriage Legislation,* p. 248.

[19] Wouters, *De Forma . . . Celebrationis Matrimonii,* p. 24, in note 1.

[20] Cronin, *op. cit.,* pp. 73, 76; Gasparri, *De Matrimonio,* 3 ed., n. 1134.

form the marriage scheduled for the morrow; he has but the one assistant (who, it is presumed, has not general delegation for marriage); he explains the situation to the assistant, gives instructions regarding the decorations for the altar, but in his excitement forgets to say, "You will assist at the marriage for me." This assistant, Vlaming observes, may validly assist at the marriage, since the necessary delegation is sufficiently implied in the actions of the pastor.[21] Vidal objects to this view as favoring tacit delegation.[22] In order to avoid serious doubts and scruples, no one should assist at a marriage unless he has explicit delegation from one empowered to delegate.

2. *Delegation May Be Given Only to a Priest*

In this requirement that the one delegated for marriage be a priest, the Code of Canon Law is only renewing the provisions of the decrees *Tametsi*, and *Ne Temere*.[23] No special qualifications are called for in the law. Hence, any priest may be delegated even though he has not been approved for confessions or assigned to parish work.[24]

3. *The Priest Delegated Must Be a Definite Priest*

Under the discipline of the decree *Tametsi*, the priest delegated could be indefinite, *e. g.*, any priest in the diocese.[25] The decree *Ne Temere* introduced the change which is contained in canon 1096, § 1. The delegated priest must be determined, must be definitely designated, and the delegator is to do the designating. When a pastor delegates, there is to be no doubt in his mind concerning the recipient of the delegation. The parties cannot be permitted to select the priest themselves nor can a third person be permitted to choose a

[21] *Praelectiones Juris Matrimonialis*, II, p. 187, note 3.

[22] Wernz-Vidal, *Jus Canonicum*, V, n. 538, p. 534, note 45.

[23] Conc. Trident., sess. XXIV, *de ref. matrimonii*, c. 1; S. C. C., *decr.*, *"Ne Temere,"* 2 August, 1907, Art. VI; *Fontes*, n. 4340.

[24] Rossi, *De Celebratione Matrimonii*, p. 99; Wouters, *De Forma . . . Celebrationis Matrimonii*, p. 29.

[25] Leitner, *Die Verlobungs—und Eheschliessungsform*, p. 46.

priest to assist at marriage. The Pontifical Commission, 20 May, 1923, declared a delegation for marriage invalid when given to a superior of a monastery thus: "I delegate for the marriage in Church N——— any religious priest whom you send to celebrate Mass in that church." [26] In this delegation the priest was not sufficiently determined for as far as the pastor is concerned he cannot say which priest will celebrate the Mass, except in a general way that *some priest* of the religious superior N———. Hence, he does not know, except in a general and indeterminate way, who will assist at the marriage. In truth, it is the religious superior who designates the priest for the marriage. Hence it is that the Commission declared that delegation given in this manner was not valid. The pastor could have given delegation to the superior of the monastery with the clause to subdelegate or he could have delegated all the religious priests of the superior N——— for a determined marriage. In delegating all the priests of the religious superior N——— for a definite marriage, the *pastor* determines the priest who will assist at the marriage. This is what is required by the law.

The delegator need not know the priest personally or by name. He may be sufficiently designated to fulfill the law by referring to his office, as the canon theologian; or to a quality by which he is known, as, the senior member of the community.[27] Likewise it is to be carefully noted that the law does not restrict delegation to *one* priest. Several may be delegated provided they are sufficiently determined by the delegator. When, however, several priests are designated to assist at a marriage, it is advised that there be some understanding as to the manner of deciding who will assist since all cannot assist at the same time. This will avoid confusion and do away with possible anxieties and doubts which may arise concerning the validity of the delegation.[28]

[26] Pontif. Comm. Inter. Cod., 20 May, 1923—*A. A. S.*, XVI (1924), 115.

[27] Gasparri, *De Matrimonio,* 4 ed., n. 950; Wernz-Vidal, *Jus Canonicum,* V, n. 538, note 41; Vlaming, *Praelectiones Juris Matrimonialis,* II, n. 573; Cappello, *De Sacramentis,* III, n. 674.

[28] Leitner, *Lehrubuch des katholischen Eherechts,* p. 203; Vlaming, *Praelectiones Iuris Matrimonialis,* II, n. 573.

4. *Delegation Can Only Be Granted for a Definite Marriage.*

Before the publication of the Code of Canon Law, delegation could be granted for marriages in general, *i. e.*, for any marriages, therefore, which might occur.[29] Under the discipline of the decree *Tametsi*, pastors were accustomed at the beginning of each year to delegate one another for all marriages in order to avoid the possible invalidity of marriage because the proper pastor had not given delegation for the marriage. The practice was tolerated under the decree *Ne Temere*, but is now rejected by the Code.[30] Delegation, therefore, must be given for a definite marriage, (for the only exception confer below). The Code does not say how a marriage is made definite but canonists consider a marriage as determined or definite; (1) by the names of the parties who are to be married; (2) or by reference to the parties through qualites or position which distinguishes them from all others;[31] (3) by reference to it as occurring at a precise hour, and day, even without the names of the parties.[32] The important point to remember is that the delegation can only be given for a proposed marriage. It cannot be given for any marriage which *may arise* in a certain parish during a certain period of time. The law does not mean to imply that a priest may be delegated for *one* marriage only. As long as the marriages are specified, definite, determined, he may be delegated for them without any question of numbers.

The law, however, allows general delegation to be granted to one class, namely, to assistants (*vicarii cooperatores*) for the parish to which they are assigned (canon 1096, § 1).[33] They may be given

[29] Chelodi, *Jus Matrimoniale*, n. 133; *S. C. de Sacramentis*, 27 July, 1908; *A. S. S.*, XLI (1908), 510-512, ad IV: "quoad delegationem nihil esse immutandum, excepta necessitate eam faciendi sacerdoti determinato ac certo, ac restrictam ad territorium delegantis."

[30] De Becker, *De Matrimonio*, p. 139; Vlaming, *Praelectiones Juris Matrimonialis*, II, n. 574, note 2.

[31] Rossi, *De Celebratione Matrimonii*, p. 101; Cance, *Le Code de Droit Canonique*, II, n. 489, note 1.

[32] Ayrinhac-Lydon, *Marriage Legislation*, p. 248.

[33] Canon 1096, § 1, is very clear in forbidding general delegation. From the words ". . . *exclusis quibuslibet delegationibus generalibus nisi agatur de vicariis*

this general delegation for marriages by the diocesan statutes, or by the local Ordinary, or by the pastor of the parish to which they have been appointed. However, if general delegation is not had from one of these sources, an assistant will be obliged, like any other priest, to be delegated expressly for each marriage.[34] The Holy Office, 7 September, 1898, declared that the faculty to administer the sacraments did not include the authority to assist at marriage, except in the case of vice-pastors who from the custom of the diocese were habitually delegated.[35] In answer to a doubt concerning the validity of marriages performed by assistants who had not received general delegation from the diocesan statutes but who assisted at marriages on the strength of the practice that it was permitted them to do so as long as the pastor did not object, the Sacred Congregation of the Sacraments replied: *"acquiescant, facto verbo cum SSmo."* [36] From this decision it would seem that the assistance rendered was doubtful at least, but the marriages were to be considered valid in virtue of a general sanction given by the Holy Father.[37] Hence, should similar cases arise in which assistants witnessed marriages because they believed themselves delegated by custom, it would seem that the situation would have to be explained to the Holy See. It is evident that if assistants are to receive general delegation for marriages in the parish of their assignment, this should be expressly stated in the diocesan statutes or made clear to the assistant by the Ordinary in his letter of appointment, or be clearly stated by the pastor of the parish.

If assistants have received delegation from the local Ordinary (and this seems to be the general practice in the United States), it would seem that the lawful use of it will require the pastor's consent. In some dioceses of this country the Ordinaries state this distinctly in the letter of appointment sent to the assistant or in the

cooperatoribus pro paroecia cui addicti sunt. . . .," it seem clear that even a Chancellor could not be given general delegation by the Bishop for marriages in the diocese.

[34] Rossi, *De Celebratione Matrimonii,* p. 99.

[35] *Coll. P. F.,* n. 2020.

[36] 10 March, 1910—*A. A. S.,* II (1910), 193-196.

[37] Wouters, *De Forma . . . Celebrationis Matrimonii,* p. 24, note 1.

diocesan Faculties. In other dioceses no mention is made of the pastor. It seems, however, that the mind of the Church on the question would certainly lean towards the necessity of the pastor's permission (at least, his implied permission). This permission has nothing at all to do with the validity of the marriage but the *lawful use* of the general delegation granted by the Ordinary is the point in question. If assistants could assist at marriages without any regard for the pastor, it could rightly be said that there were two pastors in the parish as regards marriage. In the canons which treat of the prenuptial investigation the pastor of the parties is always spoken of. Hence, it seems within the field of prudence to say that the pastor is the one who should take care of marriages in the parish. The general delegation which the Ordinary grants is intended, it seems, to prevent any doubts or anxieties about valid assistance. The lawful use of this delegation seems to require the presumed permission of the pastor. For the sake of clarity, and uniformity, it would be well if this requisite for the lawful use of general delegation were incorporated into the diocesan Faculties. It cannot be sufficiently insisted upon that *assistants alone* may receive general delegation. A missioner, working in a country which is not divided into quasi-parishes, may receive general delegation also.[38] A pastor who is without an assistant will have to use care in replacing himself as far as marriages are concerned. A priest who is helping in a parish for the summer months, unless he is appointed as a curate, must receive special delegation for each marriage which he performs.[39] In very special circumstances the Holy See may be petitioned for an indult whereby a determined pastor may delegate for marriages *ad instar cooperatoris* a priest who is not an assistant.[40]

It remains to consider some other conditions upon which the validity of delegation may depend. First of all, delegation must be freely given, as is evident from the word *expresse* (canon 1096, § 1). Delegation, however, which was given because of grave fear will very probably be valid. Canon 1095, § 1, n. 3, under pain of nullity re-

[38] *Inst.*, S. C. P. F., 25 July, 1920; *A. A. S.*, XII (1920), 331, 332.

[39] Gasparri, *De Matrimonio*, 4 ed., n. 950.

[40] *Th. Pr. Quartalschrift*, LXXVI (1923), 688; De Smet, *De Spons. et Matrimonio*, I, n. 116, note 1.

quires that the priest who assists at a marriage be free from force and fear. It says nothing about delegation obtained through fear, and from this silence, as well as from the difference between *assistance at marriage* through fear and *delegation to assist* obtained through fear, most authors defend the validity of delegation thus obtained. They argue that invalidating clauses must be strictly interpreted, and, in the absence of a clause which expressly declares that delegation is invalid, which has been obtained through coercion or force, the general principle governing the effect of grave fear must be invoked for a solution of the question. This principle holds that while grave fear lessens voluntarium it does not destroy it.[41] In the latest edition of his book on Marriage, Cardinal Gasparri changes his former view on this question, which was the same as that just stated, and now holds that delegation obtained through fear is invalid. He argues from canon 1095, § 1, n. 3, and *Regula Juris* 72, R. J. in VI°, thus if a pastor cannot validly assist at a marriage himself through fear (canon 1095, § 1, n. 3) in granting delegation under the pressure of fear, he would invalidly substitute another for himself.[42]

It may happen that the delegator made a mistake in granting delegation. What is to be said of the validity of such delegation? A substantial error will render the delegation invalid. Therefore, delegation given for marriage between Caius and Bertha will be invalid if Titus and Bertha appear before the priest delegated for the marriage.[43] Likewise, an error concerning the person delegated may make the delegation invalid; *e. g.*, if Peter is delegated, but through a mistake on the delegator's part thinking him John, the brother of the bride.[44] If the delegator, however, in this case intended to give delegation unconditionally for the marriage, it would be valid because all the conditions of canon 1096, § 1, would be observed. Moreover, if

[41] Vlaming, *Praelectiones Juris Matrimonialis,* II, n. 572; Wouters, *De Forma . . . Celebrationis Matrimonii,* p. 23; Cappello, *De Sacramentis,* III, n. 675, b; Bouuaert-Simenon, *Manuale Juris Canonici,* II, p. 304; Rossi, *De Celebratione Matrimonii,* p. 100; Payen, *De Matrimonio,* II, n. 1778.

[42] Gasparri, *De Matrimonio,* 4 ed., n. 948.

[43] S. C. S. Off., 2 August, 1899—*A. S. S.,* XXXII (1899), 191, 192.

[44] Cappello, *De Sacramentis,* III, n. 675; Gasparri, *De Matrimonio,* 4 ed., n. 948; Chelodi, *Jus Matrimoniale,* n. 133; Wouters, *De Forma . . . Celebrationis Matrimonii,* p. 23.

the pastor intended to delegate the *brother of the bride,* the delegation might be sufficiently determined in view of his intention despite the fact of a mistake of identity as to who is the brother of the bride. A simple error in names would not invalidate the delegation provided there was no mistake in the persons of the parties.[45]

An error in the quality of the parties, or delegated priest, or fraud perpetrated in the alleging of a reason for the delegation would invalidate the delegation only if it were granted on the sole condition that the facts stated were verified; in other words, if the quality in question, or the reason for the concession of the delegation were placed as a *sine qua non* condition.[46] It may be difficult at times to distinguish a warning (*monitio*) from a true condition. The context, the character of the delegator, the circumstances of the case, are some of the factors which will help to decide whether the condition prescribed is to be understood as a true condition or simply a warning. When a marriage has already been celebrated and a doubt arises regarding its validity because it is not certain whether the condition which was not fulfilled was a simple monition or a true condition—it may be considered to have been a warning (because the validity of the marriage is to be favored),[47] unless the contrary can be clearly established.

If an assistant received general delegation for a definite period of time, he must exercise care in observing the time limit lest he overrun his delegation. Common error may supply the lack of delegation if one is erroneously thought to have *general delegation.* It is at least doubtful whether supplied jurisdiction could be invoked if the error is concerned with delegation for *one* marriage. The Church intends to supply only when the community would be injured by the error.[48]

The priest who is to assist at marriage in virtue of delegation should be assured of his commission before he acts.[49] Must the priest

[45] Wouters, *De Forma . . . Celebrationis Matrimonii,* pp. 23, 24.

[46] Gasparri, *loc. cit.;* Chelodi, *loc. cit.*

[47] Gasparri, *De Matrimonio,* 4 ed., n. 957.

[48] Aertnys-Damen, *Theologia Moralis,* II, n. 836; *Periodica,* XXII (1933), 196*-200*.

[49] Gasparri, *De Matrimonio,* 4 ed., n. 952.

delegated for a marriage know of the delegation and accept it before he can validly assist? The question will not arise often for there will usually be tacit acceptance on the part of the priest delegated which is considered sufficient. Delegation granted in the presence of the delegate is tacitly accepted by his silence.[50] The petition of delegation directly or through a third person always implies acceptance.[51] This is true also if the delegatee has not formally petitioned a third person to obtain the delegation but knows that the third person is requesting delegation for him.[52] It is quite certain that delegation granted by the law of the diocese or by common law does not require acceptance in order to be valid.[53] Hence, in a diocese where delegation is granted to assistants by diocesan faculties or synodal decrees a marriage would be valid if a particular assistant witnessed it not knowing he was authorized to assist, or not thinking of the necessity of delegation.[54]

A difficulty arises in a case in which delegation is granted spontaneously by the delegator (*motu proprio*); or in the case when a third person seeks delegation for a priest who does not know of the request which has been made in his behalf. The following example will illustrate the case: Father Adrian is to assist at a marriage in a mission church and through some misunderstanding he falsely believes that he has been delegated by the pastor of the place. In the meantime a third party, realizing the difficulty of the situation, seeks delegation from the Bishop for Father Adrian, who is still unaware of the defect, but learns after assisting at the marriage that the Bishop had granted delegation a few hours before the ceremony.[55] Was the delegation valid without the acceptance of Father Adrian?

Before the Code, and even today, many authors hold that at least implied acceptance of delegation is necessary for its validity. Some

[50] "*Qui tacet, consentire videtur*"—Reg. 43, R. J., in VI°.

[51] Chelodi, *Jus Matrimoniale*, n. 133; Gasparri, *De Matrimonio*, 4 ed., n. 951.

[52] Cappello, *De Sacramentis* III, n. 675; Wernz-Vidal, *Jus Canonicum*, V, n. 538.

[53] Wernz-Vidal, *Jus Canonicum*, V, p. 634, note 46; Kearney, *Principles of Delegation*, p. 92.

[54] Ayrinhac-Lydon, *New Matrimonial Legislation*, p. 251.

[55] Kearney, *Principles of Delegation*, p. 92.

base their belief on the reason that delegation is a sort of donation (*donatio*) which must be accepted to become effective.[56] Vlaming regards acceptance as necessary to constitute the bond between the delegator and the one delegated in virtue of which the latter acts in the name of the former.[57]

For the opinion which regards Father Adrian's act as valid, a few authors quote canon 37 which says a rescript is valid if sought without the assent of him to whom it is granted.[58] The controversy gives rise to a *dubium juris*,[59] and until an authoritative decision is had on the question, the view may be followed which holds that acceptance is not necessary (canon 15).

Article III. The Use and Cessation of Delegation

The manner in which the priest who has been delegated for a marriage is to carry out his commission, and the question of the cessation of delegation are matters yet to be considered.

1. *Use of Delegation*

Because delegation for marriage means that a certain determined priest assists as the Church's qualified witness in the place of the pastor or local Ordinary, it is evident that the delegated priest will be obliged to assist in the manner prescribed for the pastor in canon 1095, § 1, § 2. It is true that the Code is silent on the manner of assisting when the delegated priest witnesses a marriage but the analogy between the pastor and delegate is very clear. The decree *Ne Temere* in Article VI said that the delegate in assisting at marriage must observe the limits of his mandate and the rules laid down for the parish priest and local Ordinary.[60] Hence, (1) the delegate must

[56] Wernz-Vidal, *Jus Canonicum*, V, p. 634, note 46, quoting D. 10, *de donatione*, XXXIX, 5.

[57] *Praelectiones Juris Matrimonialis*, II, n. 573.

[58] Cappello, *De Sacramentis*, II, n. 391; Aertnys-Damen, *Theologia Moralis*, II, n. 837.

[59] The Rota refused to declare a similar case invalid because of the gravity of this doubt, *cf.* in *Causa Divionen*, 20 January, 1911; *A. A. S.*, III (1911), 284.

[60] S. C. C., 2 August, 1907—*Fontes*, 4340.

not be excommunicated, or interdicted or suspended from office by a condemnatory or declaratory sentence (canon 1095, § 1, n. 1); (2) he must assist at the marriage within the territory of the delegator (canon 1095, § 1, n. 2); (3) he must ask and receive the consent of the parties, unconstrained by violence or grave fear (canon 1095, § 1, n. 3).[61]

A few authors consider a marriage valid even though the delegated priest were under the sentence of excommunication, suspension from office, or interdict. Their reason is that the Code is silent. These authors cite the difference between the pastor and a delegate as the official witness; the former is the *ordinary official witness,* the latter the *extraordinary* one. They believe that the Code is less exacting with the extraordinary official witness.[62] In regard to this question there would seem to be a doubt of law (*dubium iuris*) and hence, a marriage celebrated before a delegated priest who was under a sentence of excommunication cannot be absolutely declared invalid. The case would be more prudently referred to the Holy See for solution.[63]

For licit assistance at marriage the delegate must observe the conditions of canon 1097 and any further requirements which the delegator may have given.[64]

2. *Cessation of Delegation*

A particular delegation will cease when the marriage for which it was given is performed. A general delegation which an assistant receives for the parish to which he has been assigned ceases in that parish when he is officially transferred to another. The delegated priest may renounce the delegation received but the renunciation must be made known directly to the delegator and be accepted by him. The delegator (or his successor) may revoke a delegation to assist at a

[61] Payen, *De Matrimonio,* II, n. 1784; De Smet, *Betrothment and Marriage,* I, 122; Vermeersch-Creusen, *Epitome,* II, n. 396; Hyland, *Excommunication,* p. 105.

[62] *Cf.* Wouters, *De Forma . . . Celebrationis Matrimonii,* p. 25; Vlaming, *Praelectiones Juris Matrimonialis,* II, 573.

[63] Hyland, *loc. cit.*

[64] Cappello, *De Sacramentis,* III, n. 677.

marriage after it has been given. The Code, however, requires that the revocation be made known *directly* to the delegate. The recall does not take effect until the delegate is apprised of it. In the event that a pastor were removed from office, or transferred to another parish, or had died, a delegation given by him to another priest for a marriage as a rule would not expire. It would expire only in the case when the delegation contained a clause to the effect that it should cease in these circumstances.[65]

[65] Canon 207, § 1; canon 61; Gasparri, *De Matrimonio,* 4 ed., n. 958; Kearney, *Principles of Delegation,* pp. 111-116.

CHAPTER VI

LAWFUL ASSISTANCE AT MARRIAGE

Canon 1097, § 1. Parochus autem vel loci Ordinarius matrimonio licite assistunt:

1° Constito sibi legitime de libero statu contrahentium ad normam iuris;

2° Constito insuper de domicilio vel quasi-domicilio vel menstrua commoratione aut, si de vago agatur, actuali commoratione alterutrius contrahentis in loco matrimonii;

3° Habita si conditiones deficiant de quibus, n. 2, licentia parochi vel Ordinarii domicilii vel quasi-domicilii aut menstruae commorationis alterutrius contrahentis, nisi vel de vagis actu itinerantibus res sit, qui nullibi commorationis sedem habent, vel gravis necessitas intercedat quae a licentia petenda excuset.

§ 2. In quolibet casu pro regula habeatur ut matrimonium coram sponsae parocho celebretur, nisi iusta causa excuset; matrimonia autem catholicorum mixti ritus, nisi aliud particulari iure cautum sit, in ritu viri et coram eiusdem parocho sunt celebranda.

§ 3. Parochus qui sine licentia iure requisita matrimonio assistit, emolumenta stolae non facit sua, eaque proprio contrahentium parocho remittat.

WITHIN the limits of the parish or of the diocese, a pastor and local Ordinary validly assist at *all* marriages—whether the parties are their subjects or not.[1] While this was purposely intended by the framers of the decree *Ne Temere,* and incorporated into the Code in order to safeguard the validity of marriage, it must be remembered that there is a difference between valid and lawful assistance at mar-

[1] Canon 1095, § 2; *cf.* Chapter IV, Art. II.

riage and that a pastor or local Ordinary cannot *lawfully* assist at all marriages within the confines of his jurisdiction. In the interest of good order, and to prevent intrusion on parochial rights, as well as to insure a better investigation of the freedom of the parties to marriage, the Code has laid down rules governing the lawful exercise of the authority to witness marriage. These regulations are found in canon 1097 and are seriously binding upon all pastors and Ordinaries. The failure to comply with them, while grievously sinful, will not invalidate the assistance rendered provided the pastor was otherwise competent to assist validly at the marriage.

The conditions of lawful assistance concern: (1) a title to assistance; (2) permission to assist; (3) the freedom of the parties to marry; (4) the pastor of preference, and (5) refund of stole fee. Each condition will be discussed in a separate article.

Article I. Title to Lawful Assistance

A pastor assists lawfully at a marriage if one of the parties has a domicile, or quasi-domicile, or a month's residence in his parish. If one of them is a *vagus,* the pastor may lawfully assist provided the *vagus* has an actual dwelling in his parish. The same applies to the Ordinary for his diocese, and to all those who in law are included in the terms pastor and Ordinary.[2] The Code does not state this expressly in canon 1097, § 1, n. 2 but it is readily inferred. In the canon mentioned the law speaks of acquiring a domicile or quasi-domicile or month's residence *in loco matrimonii.* The Code recognizes a diocesan as well as parochial domicile and quasi-domicile (canon 92, § 3). Hence a general term, *in loco matrimonii* is used in order to embrace diocesan and parochial domicile and quasi-domicile, with their respective meanings (canon 92, §§ 1, 2). In the following pages for conciseness reference will be made only to the lawful assistance of the pastor with the understanding that the same applies to others who in virtue of canon 1094 are authorized to witness marriages. Titles to lawful assistance therefore are the following: (1) domicile or quasi-domicile; (2) a month's residence in the

[2] *Cf.* Chapter III, Art. I.

parish; (3) actual dwelling in parish, if one is a *vagus*.[3] In the present article each title will be examined.

1. *Domicile and Quasi-Domicile*

A domicile is acquired in a parish or diocese by residence therein with the intention of dwelling there always if nothing calls one away, or by actual residence in said diocese or parish for ten years (canon 92, § 1). A quasi-domicile is obtained from residence in a parish or diocese with the intention of remaining for the greater portion of the year; or by actual residence of six months (canon 92, § 2). A parochial domicile may be acquired in a quasi-parish; a diocesan domicile in a Vicariate or Prefecture Apostolic (canon 92, § 3). Domicile or quasi-domicile may be acquired from the first day one takes up residence in a place provided one has the intention of residing always or for the greater part of the year.[4] The intention may be declared expressly or be implied in one's action, *e. g.* building a house and moving into it, or leasing house for seven months and dwelling here.[5] Residence implies a permanent living place (*per modum habitantis*), not simply a place of business. It makes no difference whether one owns the house in which he is dwelling or rents it; or whether he resides in a private home or a hotel.[6] Minors retain the domicile of those under whose supervision they are placed (canon 93, § 1) but when they have outgrown their infancy they may acquire a quasi-

[3] The discipline under the decree *Tametsi* began with the recognition of domicile alone as a title to lawful assistance. Later *quasi-domicile* was admitted. The Fathers of the Third Plenary Council of Baltimore, May 12, 1886, obtained from the Holy See a declaration that residence of one month in any locality would be conclusive proof of *quasi-domicile* (Creagh, *Commentary in Decree Ne Temere*, p. 45). The decree *Ne Temere* recognized only domicile and a month's residence as titles to lawful assistance, (S. C. C. decret., *Ne Temere*, Art. V, § 2—*Fontes*, n. 4340; S. C. C. *Romana et aliarum*, 28 March, 1908, ad V—*Fontes*, n. 4349).

[4] D'Annibale, *Summula*, I, n. 83.

[5] De Smet, *De Spons. et Matrimonio*, I, n. 47; Chelodi, *Jus Matrimoniale*, n. 134.

[6] Vermeersch-Creusen, *Epitome*, I, n. 183; Wouters, *De Forma . . . Celebrationis Matrimonii*, p. 31; Wernz-Vidal, *Jus Canonicum*, II, n. 11.

domicile of their own (canon 93, § 2). Many canonists take it for granted that a minor shares the quasi-domicile of his parent or guardian [7] while others deny this because of the positive silence of the Code especially in canon 93.[8] Vermeersch admits a legal quasi-domicile for minors when the guardian or parents have only a quasi-domicile. This is permitted, he says, to prevent the minors in question from being classified as *vagi*.[9] Costello favors the opinion of Kinane and De Meester, at least in the abstract, but admits strong probability in the opinion which recognizes a legal quasi-domicile.[10]

Domicile or quasi-domicile are lost when one leaves the place of residence with the intention of not returning (canon 95). It is of importance to note that departure from a place of domicile in order to contract marriage does not carry with it the loss of domicile previous to the celebration of the marriage. This observation applies to an engaged woman who leaves her domicile in view of her approaching marriage and is restricted to a change of domicile in view of marriage. An engaged woman who has attained her majority can change her domicile if she desires,—the point mentioned concerns only a change with a view to marriage, and the reason for it is that an engaged woman leaving under the said circumstances does so conditionally, *viz.*, if the marriage takes place.[11] It is well to recall that a person may have several domiciles, *viz.*, when he resides in two or three places with the intention of residing there perpetually.[12] Authors disagree about a plurality of quasi-domiciles. Maroto states that two quasi-domiciles may be had and bases his argument upon canon 95 which says a quasi-domicile is lost when one leaves with the intention of not returning. A person may have a quasi-domicile in A, but goes to B with the intention of remaining there the greater por-

[7] Chelodi, *Jus de Personia*, n. 92; Maroto, *Institutiones* I, n. 413; Aertyns-Damen, *Theologia Moralis*, I, n. 149, pp. 107, 108, nota 6.

[8] Kinane, *I. E. R.*, 5 series, vol. 27 (1926), 81—De Meester, *Compendium*, I, n. 318, nota 7.

[9] Vermeersch-Creusen, *Epitome*, I, n. 185.

[10] Costello, *Domicile and Quasi-Domicile*, p. 177.

[11] S. R. Rotae in Causa Parisien, 5 May, 1914—*A. A. S.*, VI (1914), 397; Fourneret, *Le Domicile Matrimonial*, p. 53; Costello, *op. cit.*, p. 147.

[12] Costello, *op. cit.*, p. 154.

tion of the year having all the while the intention of returning to A.[13] Vermeersch denies that one can possess two quasi-domiciles because one cannot wish to remain for the greater part of the year in two places during the same year.[14] Costello believes that the opinion of a plurality of voluntary quasi-domiciles is more probable and may be followed in practice.[15]

In a doubt as to whether one's dwelling is in parish A or B, or in diocese A or B, the practical and more prudent procedure will be to consult the local Ordinary.[16]

2. *A Month's Dwelling*

In keeping with the decree *Ne Temere,* the Code recognizes a month's residence of one of the parties in the place of marriage as a lawful title of assistance. Under the decree *Tametsi,* in the United States after 1886, and in the diocese of Paris and Breslau after 1905 a month's dwelling gave rise to a presumption of quasi-domicile.[17] The month's residence must be complete, morally uninterrupted, and immediately prior to the marriage.

There is no restriction on persons who may acquire the month's residence. Hence it may be obtained by persons with a domicile or quasi-domicile elsewhere; likewise by *vagi,* but, as will be noted later, even though a month's residence of a *vagus* will give a title of lawful assistance to a pastor, the pastor cannot assist until he has consulted the Ordinary concerning the freedom of the *vagus* to marry (canon 1032). No intention is required in order to obtain a month's residence. The objective, external, fact of residence alone is considered as is evident from the wording of the law.[18] Likewise, there is no consideration of religion. The fact of residence is alone con-

[13] Maroto, *Institutiones,* I, n. 413. *Cf.* also Ojetti, *Commentarium,* II, p. 50, nota 46; Chelodi, *Jus de Personis,* n. 92, Cocchi, *Commentarium,* II, p. 22; Costello, *op. cit.,* pp. 155-159.

[14] *Epitome,* I, n. 185. *Cf.* also Wernz-Vidal; *Jus Canonicum,* II, n. 14; De Meester, *Compendium,* I, 319.

[15] *Op. cit.,* p. 159.

[16] Cappello, *De Sacramentis,* III, n. 680.

[17] *A. S. S.,* XXXVIII (1905), 208.

[18] Gasparri, *De Matrimonio,* 4 ed., n. 986; Wouters, *De Forma . . . Celebrationis Matrimonii,* p. 33.

templated and this in order to establish a clear and definite norm for knowing when one might lawfully assist. Hence, if a non-Catholic dwells for a month in parish A and wishes to marry a Catholic, the pastor of parish A *per se* has a title to lawful assistance at the marriage.[19] The dwelling need not be *per modum habitationis;* the Code uses the word *commoratio*. Hence, residence which involves a sojourn in a place will suffice—business, travel, as a guest, or laborer.[20] The stay spoken of is determined by a night sojourn rather than that of day. For example, if one stays in parish A each night for a month but each day is employed in parish B the month's residence will be in parish A.[21] If one works at night in parish B, and dwells in A in the day the month's dwelling will likewise be said to be in parish A.[22]

The month's dwelling must be complete, and will be calculated according to canon 33, § 3. The month will be taken as in the calendar. The first day will not be counted unless the reckoning coincides with the beginning of the first day. If the first day is not counted the month will be completed on the completion of the corresponding numerical day, *e. g.*, beginning on December 3rd, (sometime during the day) the month's residence will be completed at midnight of January 3rd (canon 33, § 3, n. 3). Should the month lack a corresponding day, *e. g.*, beginning on January 30th, it will be completed at midnight of February 28th (or 29th) (canon 33, § 3, n. 4).

The month's residence is to be continuous. However, an absence of a day or two, according to authors, will not interrupt the continuity even though one left with the intention of not returning. The *fact* of residence alone is required and this may be had without an intention of residing for any specific purpose. Since absence of a day or two very probably does not break the moral unity of the month's residence, there will not be any need of supplying them.[23]

[19] S. C. de Sacramentis, 28 January, 1916 *Fontes*, n. 2113; *cf.* Art. IV of this chapter.

[20] Rossi, *De Celebratione Matrimonii*, n. 56; Cappello, *De Sacramentis*, III, 685.

[21] Gasparri, *op. cit.*, n. 986.

[22] Wouters, *loc. cit.*

[23] S. C. de Sacramentis, 26 January, 1916—*A. A. S.*, VIII (1916), 64-66;

The month's residence must be immediately prior to the celebration of the marriage. It will not suffice that one of the parties at some previous time dwelt for a month in a parish. The computation of the month, therefore, must include the celebration of the marriage as one of its terminals. An absence of a day or two however between the completion of the month's stay and the celebration of the marriage will not destroy the title of lawful assistance. It is in this point that the pastor of domicile and quasi-domicile have an advantage over the pastor of a month's residence. The former may always assist lawfully no matter what length of time his subject has been away from his parish, provided only that they have retained their domicile or quasi-domicile; the latter loses his title to assistance once the month's residence has ceased.[24] In calculating the month's residence and its continuity the rigor of the law need not be urged. A prudent judgment should be made having as its guide the ordinary manner of computing such factors.[25]

3. *Actual Dwelling*

Canon 1097, § 1, n. 2, supplies a third title in virtue of which a pastor may assist lawfully at a marriage. It concerns a *vagus* who has an actual dwelling in the place of marriage. This actual dwelling means a fixed abode of some kind. How long must a *vagus* dwell in order that he may be said to have an actual dwelling in a place? The Code does not expressly state. It implies, however, that the length of time need not be a month for it distinguishes between a month's residence and actual dwelling (canon 1097, § 1, n. 2).[26] A few hours or the day of the marriage would not be sufficient to constitute an actual dwelling.[27] A stay of some length is required which is less than a month but sufficient to be called a residence of some

Gasparri, *De Matrimonio,* 4 ed., n. 986; Wernz-Vidal, *Ius Canonicum* V. n. 541; *Epitome,* II, n. 399; Wouters, *op. cit.,* pp. 34, 35.

[24] De Smet, *De Spons. et Matrimonio,* I, n. 127; Payen, *De Matrimonio,* II, n. 1797.

[25] Chelodi, *Jus Matrimoniale,* n. 134.

[26] Gasparri *De Matrimonio,* 4 ed., n. 989.

[27] Payen, *De Matrimonio,* II, 1798.

kind.[28] This title to assistance is had even when only one party to the marriage is a *vagus*.[29]

In regard to marriage a *vagus* is one who has no domicile, nor quasi-domicile, nor month's residence; or who is a *vagus* as far as a parochial domicile is concerned, *i. e.*, having a diocesan domicile or quasi-domicile or month's residence, but no parochial attachment.[30] It will be noticed that canon 1097, § 1, distinguishes a *vagus* who has an actual dwelling (n. 2) and a *vagus* who is constantly roaming from place to place (n. 3, *actu itinerans*). The difference between the two types seems to be only this: the *vagus* with an actual dwelling has as his proper pastor for marriage the pastor of the place in which he is residing while the *vagus itinerans* has as his proper pastor the pastor of any parish in which he stops.[31]

A practical illustration of the *vagus* of actual dwelling may be verified in the following example: an immigrant has left his native soil and arrives in New York. He has given up his domicile in his native land and is en route for a city in the West. At New York he is met by his intended wife and remains there a few weeks and wishes to be married in the parish in which he is presently dwelling. He is without domicile or quasi-domicile and likewise without a month's residence yet the pastor of the parish of actual dwelling has a lawful title to assist at the marriage because of the actual dwelling of a *vagus* in his parish. Nevertheless, because of canon 1032 regarding the freedom of *vagi* to marry, the pastor in question will of necessity be obliged to obtain the permission of the local Ordinary before assisting. The permission needed in this case, however, comes under another heading and is not concerned with the title to assistance but with the freedom of the parties to marry.

Article II. Permission to Assist

It may frequently happen that a pastor learns that he cannot lawfully assist at a marriage because the parties who wish to be mar-

28 Wouters, *De Forma . . . Celebrationis Matrimonii*, p. 34.

29 Wouters, *loc. cit.*

30 Canon 91; canon 94, § 3, and canon 1097, § 1, n. 2; Payen, *De Matrimonio*, II, n. 1798, note 1.

31 Canon 94, § 2; canon 1097, § 1, n. 3; Wernz-Vidal, *Jus Canonicum*, V, p. 637, note 55.

ried have no domicile, quasi-domicile, or month's residence in his parish, and are not *vagi* but belong to another parish. Two courses are open to him. He may send them back to their proper pastor or seek permission from their proper pastor to marry them. The subject of this article is the necessity of obtaining permission when a pastor has no lawful title to assist.

The permission which is necessary in the present case must not be confused with delegation. The pastor who is asking permission plans to assist at the marriage in his own parish and needs no delegation. He is already authorized to assist validly at all marriages in his parish (canon 1095, § 2). As a matter of fact he could not be delegated for a marriage by another pastor. The pastor of parish A could not delegate the pastor of parish B to assist at a marriage of anyone in parish B. He can give his permission, however, that persons of parish A may be lawfully married in parish B. It is this permission of which canon 1097, § 1, n. 3, speaks.

Moreover, delegation must be given expressly to a determined priest and for a determined marriage. The permission of canon 1097, § 1, n. 3, may be given in general for all marriages and in grave necessity it need not be asked at all. The pastor of parish A may have an understanding with the pastor of parish B that each other grants permission for their respective subjects to be married in parishes A or B.[32]

The Code makes two exceptions to the law which requires the permission of a proper pastor for marriage, namely (a) in the case of *vagi* who are constantly on the move from one place to another; and (b) in grave necessity.

(a) *Vagi actu itinerantes.* When persons of this class (*e. g.*, a sailor who dwells only a few days in each port, or a traveling salesman, who is constantly on the road during the entire year)[33] present themselves for marriage, the pastor needs no permission from another pastor to assist, because a *vagus actu itinerans* is never long enough in any parish to become attached to it and, hence, no one

[32] Gasparri, *De Matrimonio,* 4 ed., n. 990; Wouters, *De Forma . . . Celebrationis Matrimonii,* p. 34; Rossi, *De Celebratione Matrimonii,* n. 58.

[33] Gasparri, *De Matrimonio,* 4 ed., n. 992.

pastor has any preference over the other.[34] It must be remembered, however, that canon 1032 takes precedence over this lawful title to assistance. It does not nullify it but suspends the exercise of it until the freedom of the *vagus* to marry has been approved by the Ordinary.

(b) *Grave Necessity.* In the first place it is to be observed that this exception is very general and may be determined more precisely in local legislation. Hence the particular legislation of each diocese will have to be examined in order to have a more specific idea of what constitutes grave necessity thus excusing a pastor from seeking permission of the proper pastor of marriage.

According to Gasparri a grave necessity would be had when the asking of permission would mean a serious inconvenience to the pastor or the parties. He mentions as examples a long and arduous journey which would be necessary to obtain permission or the danger that the parties may marry civilly.[35] Others mention as examples, danger of death, lack of time to obtain the necessary permission, fear of the proper pastor who has unjustly refused to assist at the marriage, inclement weather, and lack of means of communication.[36]

It is to be carefully kept in mind that the grave necessity spoken of here does not excuse a pastor from the obligation of establishing the freedom of the parties to marry. In this regard the Holy See has issued a special instruction which will be treated in the following article. In practice, except for cases where the parties are known to the pastor personally, even in cases of grave necessity the Ordinary will have to be consulted in order to insure the freedom of the parties. Moreover, a prudent pastor will be aware of diocesan regulations in regard to the marriage of persons who are not his subjects, and, unless he has the permission of the proper pastor, he will bring the matter to the attention of the episcopal Curia.

[34] Vlaming, *Praelectiones Iuris Matrimonialis*, II, n. 580.

[35] *De Matrimonio*, 4 ed., n. 993.

[36] Creath, *Commentary in Ne Temere*, p. 47; Boudinhon, *Le Mariage et Les Fiancailles*, p. 72; Wouters, *op. cit.*, p. 35; Rossi, *De Celebratione Matrimonii*, n. 58; Payen, *De Matrimonio*, II, n. 1803; Vermeesch, *Theologia Moralis*, III, n. 796.

Article III. Freedom of Parties to Marry

According to canon 1097, § 1, the first requisite for lawful assistance is that the pastor must assure himself of the absence of any impediments to the marriage. It seems more fitting, however, to discuss this requisite after having treated of the titles to lawful assistance, for a priest will not investigate the *status libertatis* of the parties until he has assured himself that he will be in a position to witness the marriage. With this natural attitude in mind, the requisite of the freedom of the parties is treated after titles to lawful assistance.

By the freedom of the parties is understood the absence of all impediments, prohibitive and diriment. It is established in the manner directed by the Code in canons 1019-1032. It is not proposed in these pages to discuss the pre-nuptial investigation or proclamation of the banns of marriage but simply to stress the seriousness of this obligation as revealed by an Instruction of the Sacred Congregation of the Sacraments which was sent to all Ordinaries.[37] In this Instruction the Holy See directs that the investigation of the *status libertatis* is not to be neglected under the pretext of wishing to end a concubinage or in order to avoid a civil marriage. Pastors must carry out the prescriptions of the law which requires a certificate of Baptism if the parties have been baptized elsewhere (canon 1021).[38] With reference to the freedom of *vagi* and immigrants who may have acquired a domicile or quasi-domicile or month's residence the Instruction gives special attention. Canon 1032 must be strictly complied with even though a pastor may have a lawful title to assistance.[39] The marriage of immigrants, while they may not be *vagi* in the canonical sense, must be referred to the Ordinary because doubt can be easily raised as to their freedom from impediments. The only reason for assisting at their marriages without previously consulting the Ordinary will be danger of death.[40] If a person has only a month's dwell-

[37] *Inst.* S. C. de Sacramentis, 4 July, 1921—*A. A. S.*, XIII (1921), 348.

[38] *Ibidem*, n. 1.

[39] "Matrimonio vagorum de quibus in canon 91, parochus, excepto casu necessitatis, numquam assistat, nisi, re ad loci Ordinarium vel ad sacerdotem ab eo delegatum delata, licentiam assistendi obtinuerit"—Canon 1032.

[40] *Ibidem*, n. 4.

ing in the place of marriage and otherwise is without domicile or quasi-domicile, the permission of the Ordinary must be had to assist. These persons fulfill the definition of a *vagus* as given by canon 91 and, hence, in accordance with canon 1032, a pastor may not assist at their marriage without the permission of the Ordinary.[41]

Article IV. The Pastor of Preference

Very often two persons to a marriage will belong to different parishes and the question will arise which pastor should assist? *Per se* both have a lawful title to assist. The Code, however, in canon 1097, § 2, states that as a rule (*pro regula*) the pastor of the bride should assist at the marriage. This ruling is not something new. It was embodied in the decree *Ne Temere*,[42] and although not mentioned in the decree *Tametsi* it was the accepted practice.[43] This practice is but the dictate of natural courtesy that the bridegroom should go to receive the bride in her parish and not require her to seek him.[44] A note in the *Acta Sanctae Sedis* reveals that this rule was adopted in the decree *Ne Temere* at the suggestion of a parish priest, the object being to prevent disputes. Also the record of marriage would be more easily found.[45]

The law states clearly that the pastor of the bride is to receive preference in every case unless a just cause excuses.[46] Hence, he is to be preferred even though he is the bride's pastor by reason of a month's residence; even when the bride is a *vaga*.[47] The wording of the canon is very broad, *in quolibet casu.* Does this preference hold for mixed and disparate marriages in which the non-Catholic

[41] De Smet, *De Spons, et Matrimonio,* I, n. 129 (page 105, note 4); Chelodi, *Jus Matrimoniale,* n. 32; Wernz-Vidal, *Jus Canonicum,* V, n. 541, note 55.

[42] S. C. C., decret., *Ne Temere,* Art. V, § 5—*Fontes,* n. 4340.

[43] Gasparri, *De Matrimonio,* 3 ed., n. 1074; Cronin, *New Matrimonial Legislation,* p. 201; Creagh, *Commentary in decree Ne Temere,* p. 49.

[44] St. Ambrose, *De Abraham,* L. I., c. 9, n. 91—M. P. L., XIV, p. 454.

[45] *A. S. S,* XL (1907), 573, note 1.

[46] Canon 1097, § 2.

[47] Payen, *De Matrimonio,* II, n. 1805; to the contrary, McNicholas, *The New Legislation on Marriage,* p. 37.

party is the bride? A definite answer cannot be obtained from the Code for the Code is silent. It simply states that as a general rule the marriage should be celebrated before the pastor of the bride (*coram sponsae parocho . . .*). The question would seem to hinge on another question: Can a non-Catholic, (baptized or not baptized) be said to have a proper pastor with regard to marriage? Before the Code several writers maintained that the preference of the bride's pastor did not hold when the bride was a non-Catholic.[48] After the Code a few writers have maintained this position.[49] Payen distinguishes between a baptized and non-baptized non-Catholic. He does not recognize the preference of the pastor of a non-baptized party.[50] The argument of these authors if summarized indicate that the canon in question refers to Catholic marriages. Woywod notes that these are the general rule—mixed marriage the exceptions—but the law envisions what normally happens. Payen's argument is that a non-baptized person has no *parochus proprius* as, according to canon 12, the Code does not legislate for them unless the law expressly states that it obliges them also.

On the other hand there is a decision of the Sacred Congregation of the Sacraments which gives a very strong reason for believing that the pastor of a non-Catholic (baptized or not) is to be preferred. The case presented to the Congregation was as follows: a certain non-Catholic girl having a domicile in Parish B wishes to marry a Catholic having a domicile in parish L of the same archdiocese. Before the marriage the girl took a month's vacation in parish S of the same archdiocese. Here she was *baptized* (note she was baptized) and received into the Church by the pastor of parish S. Only a small part of the month's vacation remained after her entry into the Church and upon its conclusion she returned to parish B where she stayed three weeks. Thereupon she went again to parish S and on her arrival contracted the marriage before the pastor of parish S who did not receive permission to assist from the pastor of parish B. The

[48] Cronin, *New Matrimonial Legislation,* p. 298, note 1; Boudinhon, *Le Mariage et Les Fiancailles,* n. 76; Creagh, *Commentary in Ne Temere,* p. 50.

[49] Fanfani, *De Jure Parochorum,* n. 309; Woywod, *H. P. R.,* XXVIII (1928), 410; *A. E. R.,* LXII (1920), 691.

[50] *Op. cit.,* n. 1805.

pastor of parish B, regarding himself the proper pastor of the girl, brought the case before the diocesan Tribunal. The diocesan decision was adverse to the pastor of parish B. The case was submitted to the Congregation of the Sacraments.[51] The Congregation decided against the pastor of parish S because the absence of the girl from his parish for three weeks caused him to lose the title to assist lawfully in virtue of her month's residence. In the discussion of this case the opinion given by the consultor revealed, however, that the month's residence of the girl did not have to be reckoned from the date of her conversion but that the simple fact of residence, independent of her religion, sufficed to give the pastor a lawful title to assist at the marriage. This the pastor of parish B had had, the Congregation admitted, but he lost it when the girl departed for three weeks.[52] This decision forms the basis of the argument of those who say that the pastor of a non-Catholic bride should assist at the marriage, unless a just cause excuses from observing this rule. The decision was given under the decree *Ne Temere* but since the Code practically repeats the law of the decree *Ne Temere* on this point it is of service in trying to reach the correct interpretation of the law. Many conclude, accordingly that the pastor of the bride has a right to assist regardless of her religious or baptismal status.[53] The practical conclusion would seem to be that the pastor of the Catholic cannot complain in the event that the pastor of the non-Catholic bride assists at the marriage provided she had a domicile, quasi-domicile or month's residence in his parish. He will have to obtain the necessary dispensation from the Ordinary of the bridegroom and consult his pastor as to his freedom to marry. Frequently there will

[51] 26 January, 1916—*A. A. S.*, VIII (1916), 64-66.

[52] "Menstrua commoratio sponsae in paroecia S computanda ne est a die eius conversionis ad fidem catholicam, an vero ab eiusdem in paroeciam ingressu? Liquido patet sufficere, ad liceitatem, factum mere externum commorationis, praescindendo a facto conversionis sponsae in fidem catholicam. Porro voluntas legislatoris ex verbis legis petenda est iuxta illud effatum: *Legislator quod voluit expressit.* At in Decr. *Ne Temere* requiritur tantummodo menstrua commoratio alterutrius contrahentis, quin ullus sermo habeatur de eorumdem religione"—*Ibid.*, n. 4.

[53] Schenk, *Mixed Religion and Disparity of Cult*, p. 285; *A. E. R.*, LXIII (1920), 417-419; LXXVII (1928), 523, 524; LXXX (1929), 200.

be a just reason to abandon the preferment of the non-Catholic's pastor and the marriage take place before the pastor of the Catholic bridegroom. The fact of the bride being a non-Catholic will constitute such a just reason.[54] Since the Code has no explicit legislation on this point, it would seem that diocesan regulations and synodal statutes could, as they frequently do,[55] direct that a mixed marriage be celebrated before the pastor of the Catholic party.

The contents of paragraph two of canon 1097, that the pastor of the bride should assist at the marriage, imposes an obligation which must be observed. Chelodi expresses the opinion that this law has no obligatory force unless it is re-enforced by custom, or diocesan statute.[56] This view does not seem exact since the law requires a just cause to be excused from it.[57] The obligation, however, which it imposes is only light. This is evident from the wording of the law, namely, it is to be observed as a rule (*pro regula*). Then, too, it does not require grave necessity for non-observance but permits it for a *justa causa,* any reasonable cause. It must also be remembered that the pastor of the bridegroom has a lawful title to assist at the marriage. The law realizes this and, hence, is not too rigorous in giving preference to the pastor of the bride.[58]

What will be an excusing cause? "Not every little reason; but a matter of saving expenses, or any arrangements for marriage that would mean the inconvenience of either party, or the observing of local social proprieties, would be considered good reasons which will be sufficient to excuse the parties from being married by the bride's pastor. Also differences between the future bride and her pastor which would mean for the latter a severe correction, or a deep humiliation—or when the pastor of the groom is a very special friend either of the groom, or of the bride, or the parties intend to reside in the groom's parish where they wish to have the marriage ceremony, such may constitute a *causa iusta.*" [59] Or again any recognized in-

[54] Aertnys-Damen, *Theologia Moralis,* II, n. 841; Wouters, *op. cit.,* p. 35.

[55] Schenk, *op. cit.,* p. 285, in note 113.

[56] *Jus Matrimoniale,* n. 135.

[57] Cappello, *De Sacramentis,* III, n. 688 b.

[58] Gasparri, *De Matrimonio,* 4 ed., n. 994; Payen, *De Matrimonio,* II, n. 1805; Wernz-Vidal, *Jus Canonicum,* V, n. 542, note 57.

[59] McNicholas, *The New Marriage Legislation,* pp. 37, 38.

convenience which common sense would respect in such matter.[60] Among other reasons mentioned by authors are these: relationship between the pastor of the groom to either one of the parties;[61] the fact that the bride made her First Holy Communion in the groom's parish, or her parents were married there;[62] the convenience of the bridegroom's parish for a journey which is to follow the wedding;[63] the fact that the church of the bridegroom is better suited for the wedding, more commodious and the like;[64] and, as has been mentioned, the fact of the bride being a non-Catholic or *vaga*.[65]

In this matter of a just cause excusing from observing the rule prefering the pastor of the bride synodal legislation, as well as local custom will be of great assistance. The judgment of a sufficient cause, Wernz observes, ought not be left to the individuals but the Ordinary would do well to set down practical norms whereby a just cause will be easily recognized.[66] If a just reason is had for celebrating the marriage before the pastor of the bridegroom, there is no need for the pastor to explain the matter to the bride's pastor. The law distinctly states that a just cause excuses. Yet much misunderstanding will be avoided by a brief explanation and this is recommended.[67]

Which pastor is to be preferred if the bride has several proper pastors by reason of domicile, quasi-domicile, or month's residence? In such circumstances each pastor has concurrent rights and the law does not determine any order of preference. Hence the bride may choose the pastor before whom she wishes to have the marriage celebrated.[68]

[60] *A. E. R.*, LXII (1920), 691.

[61] Payen, *De Matrimonio,* II, n. 1805.

[62] Lydon, *New Matrimonial Legislation,* p. 257.

[63] Wernz-Vidal, *op. cit.*

[64] Vlaming, *Praelectiones Iuris Matrimonialis,* II, n. 581.

[65] Payen, *loc. cit.*

[66] Wernz, *Jus Decretalium,* IV, n. 188.

[67] Gasparri, *De Matrimonio*, 4 ed., n. 994; Wouters, *De Forma . . . Celebrationis Matrimonii,* p. 35; Rossi, *De Celebratione Matrimonii,* n. 59; *A. E. R.*, LXII (1920) 691,

[68] Gasparri, *op. cit.*, n. 994; Vlaming, *Praelectiones Juris Matrimonialis,* II, 582; Wouters, *op. cit.*, p. 35; Rossi, *loc. cit.*

A marriage of two Catholics who belong to different rites is to be celebrated ***in the rite of the bridegroom*** and ***before his pastor*** unless a particular law should decree otherwise (canon 1097, § 2). This is a point concerning ***lawful*** assistance. Therefore, if the pastor of the bride were to assist, the marriage would still be valid.[69] If a woman who is a Latin Catholic wishes to marry an Oriental Catholic, the canonical form of marriage must be observed (canon 1099, § 1, n. 3). It is to be noted that the substantial form must be observed even though the rite of the Oriental Catholic does not prescribe same for the validity of marriage. If the man is the Oriental Catholic the marriage will be celebrated in the Oriental rite, but before his pastor and two witnesses. Canon 1097, § 2, makes allowance for particular laws which may ordain otherwise in regard to the rite which is to be observed at marriage. The Greek Ruthenians of the United States have a particular law which directs that when they marry Catholics of a different rite, the marriage is to be celebrated ***in the rite of the bride***, and ***before her pastor***. This rule was renewed by the Sacred Congregation of the Oriental Church, March 1, 1929.[70] It was laid down in this form in the decree *Cum Episcopo*, August 17, 1914.[71]

Article V. Restitution of Stole Fee

The Council of Trent punished pastors with suspension if they assisted without permission of the proper pastor at the marriage of persons who were not their subjects.[72] This suspension was abrogated by the decree *Ne Temere*, which merely declared that pastors who assisted at marriages without the permission required by law were not entitled to the stole fee which they had accepted and must return it to the proper pastor. The decree *Ne Temere* also added that the pastor in question could be punished by the Ordinary according to the seriousness of the violation of this law.[73] The Code has

[69] Duskie, *Canonical Status of Orientals*, p. 167.

[70] Art. 30—*A. A. S.*, XXI (1929), 159.

[71] S. C. de Prop. Fide pro Negotiis R. O., Art. 30—*A. A. S.*, VI (1914), 463.

[72] Conc. Trident., sess. XXIV, *de ref. matrim.*, c. 1.

[73] S. C. C., 2 August, 1907, decret., *Ne Temere*, Art. X—*Fontes*, n. 4340.

omitted the reference to punishing the pastor and has simply stated again that the stole fee in these circumstances is to be returned to the proper pastor of the parties.[74]

Canon 1097, § 3, is an explanation of an obligation which arises from justice. The pastor who has married without permission persons who are not his subjects has no right to the stole fee. In virtue of canon 462, n. 4, assistance at marriage is a function which is reserved to the pastor and, according to canon 463, § 1, he is entitled to the honorarium which is permitted on occasion of the administration of the sacraments (canon 1507, § 1). Hence, the pastor who has assisted unlawfully is bound in conscience to make restitution immediately. This obligation would exist even though canon 1097 made no mention of it, for it is one of justice.[75] Must a pastor who has assisted in good faith make restitution of the stole fee when he learns of his error? Since he resembles a *bonae fidei possessor*, it would seem, according to the principles governing restitution, that he must return the stole fee to the proper pastor.[76] Canon 1097 in paragraph three has three points which will be considered separately; (1) who is obliged to restitution; (2) what must be restored, and (3) to whom must restitution be made.

1. *Who Is Obliged to Restitution*

The obligation of restitution by common law is restricted to a pastor who has assisted at a marriage *without the permission required by law.* The italicized words supply a key to the obligation of restitution. With this in mind the one who must make restitution is a pastor who had no title to lawful assistance. In other words, when neither of the parties at whose marriage he assisted had a domicile, quasi-domicile or month's residence in his parish and, moreover, when he had no supplied title as explained in article two of this chapter, *i. e.*, in case of grave necessity or one of the parties being a

[74] Canon 1097, § 3.

[75] Gasparri, *De Matrimonio*, 4 ed., n. 996; Vermeersch-Creusen, *Epitome*, II, n. 402; Vlaming, *Praelectiones Juris Matrimoniales*, II, n. 583; Cappello, *De Sacramentis*, III, n. 689, note 30; Lydon, *Matrimonial Legislation*, p. 259; Cronin, *New Matrimonial Legislation*, p. 203.

[76] *Cf.* Aertnys-Damen, *Theologia Moralis*, I, n. 749.

vagus actu itinerans he is bound to restitution. On the other hand, however, if the pastor of the groom assisted at the marriage, he need not make restitution since he already has a lawful title to assistance (canon 1097, § 1, n. 3).[77] Likewise a pastor who assisted at a marriage of persons who were not his subjects but who was excused from seeking permission because of a grave necessity (canon 1097, § 1, n. 3) need not return the offering which was made to him for he assisted at that marriage *lawfully*. Likewise any pastor of domicile, quasi-domicile, month's dwelling, or actual dwelling in case of a *vagus*—has a legitimate title to assist at the marriage of the persons concerned; hence he is excluded from the class of those who assist *sine licentia iure requisita*.[78]

Paragraph three of canon 1097 speaks only of "pastors." What of others, *e. g.*, assistants with general delegation, who assist without the necessary permission required by law? Wouters states that they are not obliged to refund the stole fee, because penal laws are to be strictly interpreted.[79] The opinion, however, which states that other priests are obliged seems preferable. Canon 1097, § 3, is not penal in its nature but merely explains and urges an obligation of justice. The word "pastor" is used very probably because he is the ordinary official witness. It does not mention the local Ordinary but surely he would equally be obliged to refund the stole fee if he violated the right of another in this matter. It seems more in keeping with the justice due the proper pastor to say that all priests who unlawfully assist are obliged to refund the fee received.[80] The question will be for the most part impractical because the assistant usually will give the stole fee to the pastor and he will be obliged to restitution once he learns of the injustice done.

2. *What Is to Be Returned*

A stole fee is an offering which is made to the minister on the

[77] *Cf.* particular legislation may vary in this regard.

[78] Ferry, *Stole Fees*, p. 75; Gasparri, *op. cit.*, 996; Wouters, *De Forma . . . Celebrationis Matrimonii*, p. 36; Payen, *De Matrimonio*, II, n. 1805.

[79] *Op cit.*, p. 36.

[80] Cappello, *De Sacramentis*, III, n. 689; Lydon, *Matrimonial Legislation*, p. 259.

occasion of certain priestly functions.[81] The accepted amount will be stipulated by a provincial Council, or by the Bishops of an ecclesiastical province, or by legitimate custom (canon 1507, § 1).

The stole fee which must be returned will be the usual offering given on the occasion of marriage in accordance with the accepted practice. It does not include the stipend for Mass nor a gift which may be given at the time of the marriage and which was prompted by a spirit of liberality or friendship.[82] The stole fee which must be restored is understood to be a stole fee which has been actually received. Hence, normally speaking, if a pastor has assisted unlawfully and has not received anything from the parties he will not be held to any restitution.[83] Should a pastor willfully neglect to accept the stole fee, and at the same time realize that he is thereby depriving the proper pastor of it, it would seem that he should refund the amount for, as Vlaming says, his action is the equivalent of releasing someone from paying a just debt to a third person.[84] If the pastor fraudulently induced the parties to give him the offering under another pretext, *e. g.*, as a gift, or a stipend for Mass, it will be necessary for him to refund it to the proper pastor because he has virtually received it.[85]

Who is to receive the stole fee when a pastor gives permission for the lawful celebration of a marriage in another parish, according to canon 1097, § 1, n. 3? Or when he delegates another to assist at a marriage in his own (the delegator's) parish? Ferry is of the opinion that the mere granting of permission does not include a release from the stole fee.[86] Lydon would call for an understanding between the pastors concerned. If permission is given on condition that the fee is to be returned it must be returned. If the pastor makes no reservations there will be no obligation of refunding the

81 Ferry, *Stole Fees*, p. 2.

82 Gasparri, *De Matrimonio*, 4 ed., n. 996; Wernz-Vidal, *Jus Canonicum*, V, n. 542; Wouters, *op. cit.*, p. 36; Ferry, *op. cit.*, p. 78; Vlaming, *Praelectiones Juris Matrimonialis*, II, n. 583.

83 Wouters, *De Forma . . . Celebrationis Matrimonii*, p. 36.

84 *Praelectiones Juris Matrimonialis*, II, n. 583.

85 Aertnys-Damen, *Theologia Moralis*, II, n. 841; Cappello, *De Sacramentis*, III, n. 689, 6.

86 *Op. cit.*, p. 78.

honorarium since the Code is silent about such obligation.[87] In practice, local legislation, and custom will frequently supply a solution to this question.

3. *To Whom Is Restitution to Be Made*

In canon 1097, § 3, the law directs that the stole fee should be handed to the "proper pastor of the parties." Nothing more is added. If the parties have one and the same proper pastor, the one to receive the fee is easily known. If they have different proper pastors it would seem that the pastor of the bride should be preferred. By canon 1097, § 2, he is given preference over the others.[88] If there are several proper pastors, the solution would seem to be to divide the stole fee among them. There is no norm in canon 1097 for this situation and the suggestion of equal distribution is taken from a law concerning funerals (canon 1236, § 2) according to which an offering for a funeral celebrated by one who was not the proper pastor is to be divided among the proper pastors.[89] Some authors would disqualify the pastor of a month's residence from a share because he is not a *parochus proprius* in the strict sense of canon 91.[90] Others, however, argue convincingly that the pastor of a month's residence is entitled to his share. The restitution is made to one who had a right to assist and the pastor of a month's residence had as much right as the others to witness the marriage.[91] Vermeersch would restore the stole fee under these circumstances to the pastor before whom the marriage would have been celebrated.[92] In most instances, however, local custom or diocesan regulations will dictate what should be done.[93]

[87] Lydon, *Matrimonial Legislation*, p. 259.

[88] Gasparri, *op. cit.*, n. 996; Forry, *Stole Fees*, p. 77; Cappello, *De Sacramentis*, III, n. 689.

[89] Wouters, *op. cit.*, p. 36.

[90] Gennari, *Commento sul decreto Ne Temere*, p. 41; Gasparri, *De Matrimonio*, 4 ed., n. 996; Cappello, *De Sacramentis*, III, n. 689.

[91] Chelodi, *Ius Matrimoniale*, n. 135, note 3; Rossi, *De Celebratione Matrimonii*, n. 61; Vlaming, *op. cit.*, II, n. 583.

[92] *Theologia Moralis*, III, n. 796.

[93] Cappello, *loc. cit.*

CHAPTER VII

THE SUBJECT OF THE FORM OF MARRIAGE

Canon 1099, § 1. Ad statutam superius formam servandam tenentur:

1. Omnes in catholica Ecclesia baptizati et ad eam ex haeresi aut schismate conversi, licet sive hi sive illi ab eadem postea defecerint, quoties inter se matrimonium ineunt;

2. Iidem, de quibus supra, si cum acatholicis sive baptizatis sive non baptizatis etiam post obtentam dispensationem ab impedimento mixtae religionis vel disparitatis cultus matrimonium contrahant;

3. Orientales, si cum latinis contrahant hac forma adstrictis.

§ 2. Firmo autem praescripto § 1, n. 1, acatholici sive baptizati sive non baptizati, si inter se contrahant, nullibi tenentur ad catholicam matrimonii formam servandam; item ab acatholicis nati, etsi in Ecclesia catholica baptizati, qui ab infantili aetate in haeresi vel schismate aut infidelitate vel sine ulla religione adoleverunt, quoties cum parte acatholica contraxerint.

Following the division of canon 1099 this chapter will comprise two articles: the first, treating of persons bound by the canonical form of marriage; the second, persons who are exempt from it.

Article I. Persons Subject to the Canonical Form

From canon 1099, § 1, it is clear that the canonical form of marriage must be observed: (1) by persons baptized in the Catholic Church; (2) by those who have been converted to the Catholic Church from heresy or schism. They must always observe the form, even though they have later fallen away and left the Church.

They are obliged by it if they are to marry among themselves, also if they are to marry a person who *per se* is exempt from the law. The reason for the former provision, *i. e.,* being held even after apostasy, is clear. It is not fitting that these persons in case of defection should profit by their rebellion or neglect.[1] Concerning the second statement, that they are held when they marry someone *per se* exempt, a slight explanation is in order. By this law the Code removed the last vestige of the communication of exemption, a principle which held sway since the time of Benedict XIV. As has been explained in another chapter [2] with regard to the decree *Tametsi,* if one party to a marriage was exempt, (*i. e.,* in virtue of Benedictine Declaration) it was accepted that the exempted person conferred exemption on the one who was *per se* held to observe the Tridentine law. In other words, a person obliged by the law was freed from it if he married one who was not held.[3] The decree *Ne Temere* practically abrogated this principle. It obliged those who were held by the law, even when they wished to marry someone who was exempt from it. This, however, admitted exceptions.[4] The Sacred Congregation of the Council soon declared what the exception was. It was the Constitution *Provida* which Pius X had granted to Germany in 1906.[5] The Congregation in its reply made it clear that the *Ne Temere* decree had abolished the Benedictine Declaration.[6] The exemption given for the German Empire was later extended to the Kingdom of Hungary.[7] In these countries mixed marriages were valid even if the decree *Ne Temere* had been neglected for the old principle of exemption was admitted and thus

[1] Gasparri, *De Matrimonio,* 4 ed., n. 1020.

[2] Chapter II, Art. II.

[3] Gasparri, *De Matrimonio,* 4 ed., n. 1020; Creagh, *Commentary in decree Ne Temere,* p. 72.

[4] " . . . nisi pro aliquo particulari loco aut regione aliter a Sancta Sede sit statutum . . . " S. C. C., decret., *Ne Temere,* 2 August, 1907, Art. XI, § 2—*Fontes,* n. 4340.

[5] *Cf.* chapter II, Art. II.

[6] S. C. C., *Romana et aliarum,* 1 February, 1908, ad IV—*Fontes,* n. 4344. *Cf.* Creagh, *Commentary in decree Ne Temere,* p. 73.

[7] S. C. de Sacram., 27 February, 1909; A. K. K. R., LXXXIX (1909), 717-724.

the Catholic party was released.[8] Two interpretations were given concerning the Constitution *Provida* which limited its application; the first, issued 28 March, 1908, stated that the exemption was enjoyed only by those who had been born in Germany and when they contracted marriage there;[9] the second, given on 8 June, 1909, declared that both parties had to be born in Germany or in Hungary. In a marriage between a person born in Germany and one born in Hungary the form had to be observed. If neglected, the marriage was invalid.[10] These exceptions should be kept in mind by Diocesan Tribunals in certain petitions of nullity on the ground of neglect of form.[11]

The Code abrogated the principle of exemption in its entirety. It admits of no exceptions. If a person is held by the canonical form he is obliged by it always and in marrying one *per se* exempt he communicates his obligation. Hence, non-Catholics are indirectly held by the canonical form. This principle is more in accord with the individual character of the marriage contract which requires that both parties to it be capable of entering marriage. It is more in accord also with the law of the canonical form which does not cease because one person is *per se* exempt from it.[12]

At this point it is necessary to note a very special exception to the first class of persons named above (baptized in the Catholic Church). Even though a person has been baptized in the Catholic Church, the law admits of exemption under special circumstances. Later it will be necessary to examine this group in detail. For the present, the exception is merely mentioned: they are persons born of non-Catholic parents or of a mixed or disparate marriage who, although baptized in the Catholic Church, have been raised from infancy in heresy,

[8] De Smet, *De Spons. et matrimonio,* I, n. 143.

[9] S. C. C., 28 March, 1908, ad III—*A. S. S.,* XLI (1908), 288.

[10] S. C. de Sacr., 8 June, 1909—*A. A. S.,* I (1909), 516.

[11] *Cf.* Wouters, *De Forma . . . Celebrationis Matrimonii,* pp. 49-54, for a lengthy interpretation and application of the exceptions. *Cf.* also *Jus Pontificium,* X (1930), 36 ss.

[12] *Votum Consultoris,* S. C. C., 28 March, 1908—*Anal. eccl.,* XVII (1908), 121—De Smet, *De Spons. et Matrimonio,* I, n. 141; Gasparri, *De Matrimonio,* 4 ed., n. 1021.

schism, infidelity, or without any religion, and marry non-Catholics.[13]

The canonical form of marriage obliges only members of the Latin Church. Uniate Orientals (Syriacs, Armenians, Copts, etc.) are held only when they contract marriage with Latins (canon 1099, § 1, n. 3). This is because of the individual character of the marriage contract.[14] To the general statement regarding the exemption of Uniate Orientals one exception will be treated in detail at the end of this article. This exception concerns the Uniate Greek Ruthenians in certain countries who are held to the decree *Ne Temere.*

With these preliminary remarks it will be possible to discuss more in detail the persons who are subject to the canonical form of marriage.

1. *Baptized in the Catholic Church*

The designation "baptized in the Catholic Church" describes persons who are baptized with the intention of associating themselves with or being incorporated into the Roman Catholic Church. It differentiates Baptism which is received in the Catholic Church from Baptism administered in sects opposed to or not in accord with Rome. The distinction is canonical, rather than real, since every *validly* baptized person,—no matter who has administered the sacrament, heretic, or pagan,—is by the reception of valid Baptism baptized into the Catholic Church. There is but one true Church and one Baptism.[15] The distinction arises from the difference which may exist between the *finis operis* in Baptism, and the *finis operantis.*[16]

In determining who are baptized in the Catholic Church it will be necessary to keep in mind: the intention of parents or guardians with regard to infants; the intention of the person himself if he is an adult; and, occasionally, the intention of the one administering the sacrament.[17] As baptized in the Catholic Church are reckoned

[13] Canon 1099, § 2.

[14] S. C. C., *Romana et aliarum,* 1 February, 1908, ad I and III—*Fontes,* n. 4344; S. C. C., 28 March, 1908—*Fontes,* n. 4349; Gasparri, *De Matrimonio,* 4 ed., n. 1022.

[15] Conc. Trident., sess. VII, *de baptismo,* canons 7, 8; Gasparri, *De Matrimonio,* 4 ed., n. 568.

[16] Cappello, *De Sacramentis,* III, n. 410.

[17] Schenk, *Mixed Religion and Disparity of Cult,* p. 104.

primarily infants who by the will of their parents or guardians are brought to the Catholic Church for Baptism or who, being born of Catholic parents, have in the case of necessity been baptized by a lay person. The parents are the natural interpreters of the child's intentions who in the age of infancy cannot determine it.[18] The intention of parents or guardians need not be explicit. An interpretative intention will suffice and will prevail even in the event that the minister of the sacrament intended to baptize the infant in a sect other than that of the parents.[19] Adults, *i. e.*, those who at the moment of Baptism enjoy the use of reason, are said to be baptized in the Catholic Church when they present themselves to a Catholic priest in order to be baptized.[20]

An infant of heretical, schismatical, or infidel parents, may be lawfully baptized against the parents wishes if it is prudently foreseen that the infant may die before it attains the use of reason.[21] If there is due provision for their Catholic education, a Catholic may lawfully baptize the infants of infidels, schismatics, heretics, and fallen away Catholics provided: that at least one of the parents or guardians consent; or that at the time of Baptism the child has no parents, grandparents, or guardians, or that they have lost their right over the child or cannot in any way exercise it.[22] Infants baptized lawfully according to these rules are baptized in the Catholic Church and *per se* obliged to the canonical form of marriage.[23] *Per accidens*, such children may be exempted if they are reared outside the Church from infancy.[24]

What is to be said if an infant is unlawfully baptized in the Catholic Church, *i. e.*, contrary to the provisions of canon 750, §§ 1, 2, and 751? A case may be supposed of an over zealous Catholic who

[18] Thomas Aquinas, *Summa Theol.*, III a, q. 68, Art. 10, resp.

[19] Gasparri, *De Matrimonio*, 4 ed., n. 570; Schenk, *Mixed Religion and Disparity of Cult*, p. 105.

[20] Canon 745, § 2, n. 2.

[21] Canon 750, § 1.

[22] Canon 750, §§ 1, 2; canon 751.

[23] S. C. de P. F., 1 April, 1922—N. R. T., LII (1925), 497, 498; A. K. K. R., CVII (1927), 179, 180; Gasparri, *De Matrimonio*, 4 ed., n. 572, 573; Wouters, *op. cit.*, p. 47.

[24] Canon 1099, § 2.

baptizes a child outside the danger of death against the wishes of its parents or without their knowledge. For all practical purposes the solution of this question will depend upon the future religious education of the child. If he is educated in heresy, schism, infidelity or without any religion from infancy, it is quite clear that he will be exempted by canon 1099, § 2.[25] If on the contrary, the infant grows up in the Catholic religion, he would seem to be held by the form of marriage since his baptism plus his formal acceptance of Catholicism will place him in a class equivalent to that of a convert, hence he will be a subject of canon 1099, § 2. The above is especially true when the intention of the parents or guardian of the child as to what sect or Church they wished to have their child baptized is unknown. In doubt concerning their wishes, the child will be considered baptized in the Catholic Church. But if it is clearly known and understood that the parents of the child are, *e. g.*, Anglicans, and would wish their child baptized as an Anglican, it seems that a child of such parents is to be considered as baptized outside the Catholic Church even though the intention of the one unlawfully baptizing was to baptize in the Catholic Church. This is the opinion of Cardinal Gasparri and it is in keeping with what has been said concerning the right of the parents to interpret the will of their child.[26] With this opinion in mind the following case may be imagined. A child who has been unlawfully baptized unknown to his Anglican parents grows up and later neglects the practices of the Anglican Church, attends a Catholic boarding school, takes instructions in the Catholic religion with a view to becoming a Catholic, but through some reason or other never becomes a Catholic. Would he be held to the canonical form? It seems not, if the view expressed by Cardinal Gasparri is accepted, since the provisions of canon 1099, § 2, presuppose baptism received in the Catholic Church. The person in this case, due to the baptism conferred unlawfully against the wishes of his parents, was never baptized in the Catholic Church; hence, no amount of in-

[25] *Cf.* case in *Periodica* XXI (1932), 14-16, in which the Holy Office declared a child of a mixed marriage, baptized in infancy unknown to the non-Catholic parent, and subsequently reared outside of the Church exempt from the form of marriage.

[26] Gasparri, *De Matrimonio,* 4 ed., n. 570 b.

struction or preparation will make him a subject of the form of marriage. The question is not certain, for there are authors who would consider his baptism, although unlawful, as a baptism in the Catholic Church. In view of his subsequent education he would seem to be held by the form. The prudent procedure would be to refer the case to Rome.[27]

A doubt concerning a person's baptism in the Catholic Church (and his subsequent obligation of observing the form of marriage) will be settled by the usual principles governing doubts of fact or law and especially by consideration of his Catholic education and training. Frequently an exemption from the form will be afforded by canon 1099, § 2. If the person in question has already contracted marriage with a non-Catholic and is now seeking a declaration of nullity because of the lack of form, his marriage will of necessity stand as valid (canon 1014) until it is clearly established that he was baptized in the Catholic Church and a subject of the canonical form.[28]

2. *Converts to the Catholic Church from Heresy and Schism*

A convert in the sense of canon 1099, § 1, n. 1, is one who at sometime in his life prior to marriage changed from non-Catholic belief to the Catholic Faith or returned to it from schism. An infidel who has been received into the Catholic Church is likewise a convert but is classified under the group embracing those baptized in the Catholic Church. Usually a conversion takes place after one has been instructed in the teachings of the Catholic Church. A convert may be baptized absolutely or conditionally according to the circumstances of the case.

Converts are always bound to observe the canonical form of marriage even in the event that later they leave the Church and lapse into heresy or schism, or unbelief (canon 1099, § 1, n. 1). Blat seems to imply that fallen away Catholics (whether they were always Catholics, or converts) are not bound by the form when they marry non-Catholics. In the first number of canon 1099, § 1, Blat would dis-

[27] Schenk, *Mixed Religion and Disparity of Cult,* p. 108.

[28] Vermeersch-Creusen, *Epitome,* II, n. 407; De Smet, *De Spons. et Matrimonio,* I, n. 140.

tinguish two phrases; (a) Omnes in catholica Ecclesia baptizati et ad eam ex haeresi aut schismate conversi; (b) licet sive hi sive illi ab eadem postea defecerint. The provisions of the next number of canon 1099, § 1, *i. e.*, "iidem de quibus supra si cum acatholicis . . . " is to be restricted, according to Blat, to those included in the first phrase (a). Hence fallen away Catholics are not bound by the form when they marry non-Catholics.[29] This interpretation, however, is contrary to the generally accepted view of canonists,[30] and not in keeping with the principle that apostates should not profit by their defection.

According to some authors infants, who have been *validly* baptized but outside the Catholic Church, are to be considered as converts when their parents embrace the Catholic Religion. The basis of this opinion is that the parents are the natural interpreters of the infant's wishes, or that the will of the infant is included in that of their parents or guardians.[31] Other authors make the conversion of children of converts tentative on the condition that they are raised in the Catholic religion once they have acquired the use of reason. If a child objects to embracing the Catholic religion which his convert parents would impose upon him, there is no question of conversion.[32] Practically the question will have to be decided according to the training and education which such a child has received from infancy. If his convert parents have had him rebaptized in the Catholic Church, or have sent him to a Catholic school and he has received the Sacraments, all agree that he is a Catholic and held by the canonical form. Should the infant's parents apostatize before he reaches the age of reason and he is subsequently raised outside the Church, he will be

[29] For further elaboration of this argument confer Blat, *Commentarium* III, n. 501.

[30] Gasparri, *De Matrimonio*, 4 ed., n. 1020; Vermeersch-Creusen, *Epitome*, II, n. 407; Cappello, *De Sacramentis*, III, n. 700; *Apollinaris*, III (1930), 661 ss.

[31] Schenk, *Mixed Religion and Disparity of Cult*, p. 115; Augustine, *Commentary*, V, p. 300.

[32] Vermeersch-Creusen, *Epitome*, II, n. 344; Chelodi, *Jus Matrimoniale*, n. 138; Vlaming, *Praelectiones Juris Matrimonialis*, II, n. 598; Gasparri, *De Matrimonio*, 4 ed., n. 1020.

exempt according to canon 1099, § 2.[33] If only one parent has been received into the Church, the same principle will be applied. In serious doubt concerning the sufficiency of the education received in the Catholic Church the case will be more prudently sent to the Holy Office for solution. If a child has already reached the age of reason, but is still not of the age of puberty when his parents enter the Catholic Church, it is very probable that he will be considered as a convert provided: that he does not reject the Catholic religion, but is educated in it. These children are thought to wish what their parents or guardians desire.[34] In practice most of these difficulties will be obviated in as much as the priest who receives non-Catholic parents into the Church will see to the proper conversion and instruction of their children.

SCHOLION I. GREEK RUTHENIANS AND THE DECREE *Ne Temere*.—As has been mentioned, Oriental Catholics (Uniates) are not bound by the canonical form except when they contract marriage with Latins.[35] The Greek Ruthenians, however, in certain countries are under the legislation of the *Ne Temere* decree. It seems advisable to treat briefly the historical background of this question.

The decree *Ne Temere* did not mention Orientals, and *per se*, it did not oblige them as it was a disciplinary measure and intended for the Latin Church.[36] The Congregation of the Council declared that Orientals were only obliged by the decree *Ne Temere* when they married Latins.[37] The Greek Ruthenians in certain dioceses followed the legislation of the decree *Ne Temere* from the time of its publication. The Holy See later approved of the practice for the Greek Ruthenians in the province of Galacia. The reason for this was because the Ruthenian Bishops in Galacia had put the *Ne Temere* decree into effect before the Congregation had declared that Orientals were not

[33] The Commission of Interpretation has declared that the words "*ab acatholicis nati*" of canon 1099, § 2, include children whose parents have apostatized. *Cf.*, Art. II of this Chapter.

[34] Augustine, *Commentary* V, p. 299; Chelodi, *Jus Matrimoniale*, n. 138; Vlaming, *op cit.*, II, n. 598.

[35] Canon 1099, § 1, n. 3.

[36] Ferreres, *Los Esponsales y el Matrimonio*, n. 509; S. C. C., *Romana et aliarum*, 1 February, 1908, ad 1um—*Fontes*, n. 4344.

[37] S. C. C., *Romana et aliarum*, 28 March, 1908, ad 1um—*Fontes*, n. 4349.

obliged by it.[38] The Bishop of the Greek Ruthenian rite in the United States made a request of the Holy See that for the sake of uniformity of discipline the decree *Ne Temere* should be extended to all Uniate Greek Ruthenians in this country.[39] When the Holy See reorganized the status of Greek Ruthenians in the United States the decree *Ne Temere* was embodied in the new legislation.[40] The Greek Ruthenians in Canada [41] and in South America [42] are likewise governed by the decree *Ne Temere.*

Hence Greek Ruthenians in the above named countries must contract marriage under the pain of nullity before a pastor, or Ordinary or delegated priest, and two witnesses as expressed in the decree *Ne Temere.* This canonical form obliges these Greek Ruthenians when they marry among themselves, and when they contract with other Orientals heretics or schismatics. This legislation is still in force in the United States.[43]

SCHOLION II. MARONITES AND ITALO-GREEKS. According to a decree of the synod of Mount Lebanon (1736) clandestine marriages were declared invalid and it was stated that marriage must be contracted in the presence of the pastor or Ordinary or delegated priest and two witnesses.[44] The acts and decrees of this synod were approved by Pope Benedict XIV.[45] Hence it is that the decree *Tametsi* obliged the Maronites, not in virtue of publication, but because of approval by the Apostolic See of the decrees and acts of the synod of Lebanon. The binding force of the decree *Tametsi* upon Maronites

[38] S. C. de Prop. Fide pro Negotiis R. O., 21 May, 1911—A. K. K. R., XCII (1911), 484.

[39] Duskie, *Canonical Status of Orientals in United States,* p. 165.

[40] Decret., S. C. de Prop. Fide pro Negotiis R. O., 17 August, 1914, Art. 30—*A. A. S.,* VI (1914), 463.

[41] Decret., S. C. de Prop. Fide pro Negotiis R. O., 19 August, 1913, Art. 36—*A. A. S.,* V (1913), 398.

[42] Decret., S. C. de Prop. Fide pro Negotiis R. O., 27 March, 1916, Art. 17—*A. A. S.,* VIII (1916), 107.

[43] S. C. Ecc., Orient., 21 June, 1924—Letter of Apostolic Delegate to Ordinaries in the United States, August, 1924—Duskie, *op. cit.,* p. 166, in note 81; 1 March, 1929—*A. A. S.,* XXI (1929), 159.

[44] *Acta et Decreta,* pars II, cap. XL, n. XII—*Coll. Lac.,* II, 166; pars II, cap. XI, n. 28—*Coll. Lac.* II, n. 178.

[45] Const., *Singularis,* 1 September, 1741, § 10—*Coll. Lac.,* II, 488 ss.

today will be determined by the principles of interpretation which formerly governed the decree *Tametsi*. It is territorial, obliging those living in native places of Maronites. It is personal and follows a subject until he acquires a domicile or quasi-domicile outside his native place. Once a domicile or quasi-domicile is acquired, a Maronite, in a place in which the decree *Tametsi* does not bind, is released from its force.[46]

Clement VIII introduced the decree *Tametsi* among the Italo-Greeks,[47] and Benedict XIV maintained the same legislation.[48] It would seem that the Italo-Greeks are still under the provisions of the decree *Tametsi;* because on the one hand Orientals were exempt from the *Ne Temere* decree,[49] and likewise by the Code,[50] and on the other, there have been no decrees of the Holy See similar to the decrees regarding Greek Ruthenians. Accordingly, regarding the canonical form of marriage it seems that the status of the Italo-Greeks, who are Orientals, remains as it originally was. The application of the decree *Tametsi* to Italo-Greeks will follow the principles enunciated for the Maronites.[51]

Article II. Persons Who Are Exempted from the Canonical Form

The persons who are not obliged to the canonical form of marriage may be grouped into four classes: (1) infidels; (2) heretics and schismatics; (3) Catholic Orientals; and (4) a special class of persons baptized in the Catholic Church. Each group will be considered separately. One condition essential to the exemption of these persons is this: *they are exempt only when they marry among themselves.* If they marry any person belonging to the classes mentioned in the preceding article the exemption ceases. They are held then in virtue of canon 1099, § 1, n. 2 and, because of the individual char-

46 Duskie, *Canonical Status of Orientals in United States*, pp. 159-162.

47 Instr., *Sanctissimus*, 21 August, 1595, § 5—*Fontes*, n. 179.

48 Const., *Etsi Pastoralis*, 26 May, 1742, § VIII, n. I—*Coll. P. F.*, n. 338.

49 S. C. C., 1 February, 1908, ad I—*Fontes*, n. 4344.

50 Canon 1099, § 1, n. 3.

51 Duskie, *op. cit.*, p. 163.

acter of the marriage contract which exacts that for a valid marriage both parties must be free to marry. The law of the canonical form directly obliges the Catholic party and in binding him indirectly holds the exempted person.

1. *Infidels*

In as much as the Church does not legislate for non-baptized, infidels are outside of the binding force of the canonical form.[52] Catechumens are to be reckoned as infidels.[53]

2. *Heretics and Schismatics*

By heretics and schismatics are understood validly baptized persons but baptized outside the Catholic Church in heresy or schism and never converted. Baptized non-Catholics are held by ecclesiastical law unless expressly exempted.[54] The decree *Ne Temere* expressly exempted baptized non-Catholics,[55] and the Sacred Congregation of the Council declared that schismatics and heretics of the Oriental rites were included in the class of non-Catholics.[56] The Code exempts baptized non-Catholics from the observance of the form of marriage when they marry among themselves (canon 1099, § 2). In accordance, therefore, with the decision of the Sacred Congregation of the Council already mentioned, baptized non-Catholics will embrace baptized Protestants, schismatics, and heretics of the Oriental rites. Two baptized Protestants of whatever belief or two schismatics may marry validly before a judge or minister. *Per se* they would not be obliged to observe the civil form of marriage. On the one hand baptized non-Catholics are expressly exempted from the Church law concerning the form of marriage (canon 1099, § 2); and on the other, the civil law cannot legislate for the marriage of baptized persons (canon 1016). For these baptized non-Catholics

[52] Canon 12; canon 1099, § 2.

[53] Payen, *De Matrimonio,* II, n. 1843.

[54] Canon 87.

[55] S. C. C., decret., *Ne Temere,* 2 August, 1907, Art. XI, § 3—*Fontes,* n. 4340.

[56] S. C. C., *Romana et aliarum,* 28 March, 1908, ad IIum—*Fontes,* n. 4349.

the only requirements as regards the celebration of marriage will be freedom of parties to marry and mutual matrimonial consent properly exchanged; and where there exists no obstacle to their marriage, informal marriages of such baptized non-Catholics will be valid.[57]

3. *Catholic Orientals*

The decree *Ne Temere,* did not contain any reference to Orientals. Shortly after its promulgation, the Sacred Congregation of the Council declared that Orientals were only held to the decree *Ne Temere,* when they married Latins.[58] This answer was incorporated into the Code of Canon Law (canon 1099, § 1, n. 3). Catholic Orientals, therefore, are not obliged by the canonical form when they marry members of other Uniate rites, *e. g.,* Copts, Armenians, etc.[59] Likewise they are not held when they marry schismatics or heretics. The exception of Greek Ruthenians has already been noted.

4. *Certain Persons Who Have Been Baptized in the Catholic Church*

In the preceding article it has been said that persons who were baptized as Catholics must observe the canonical form. To this class, however, one exception must be made—an exception of great importance; namely, in regard to those who were born of non-Catholic parents and who, although baptized as Catholics, have since infancy been raised outside the Church. These persons are exempted by canon 1099, § 2, when they wish to marry a non-Catholic. In the decree *Ne Temere,* however, no mention was made of exempting this class of persons as the Code does in canon 1099, § 2. In 1911 the Holy Office was asked what should be done concerning the marriage of non-Catholics and those constituting this class of baptized Catholics when the canonical form of the decree *Ne Temere* was not observed. Were such marriages valid? The reply of the Holy Office di-

[57] *Jus Pontificium,* IX (1929), 171.

[58] S. C. C., *Romana et aliarum,* 28 March, 1908, ad I—*Fontes,* n. 4349.

[59] The Holy See is very strict in exempting Orientals. *Cf.* a decision of the Holy Office which upheld a marriage between two Uniates although the woman had been brought up in the Latin rite from the age of five—*A. E. R.,* LXXIII (1925), 305.

rected that the Holy See be consulted in each case.[60] In view of this instruction it would seem that should cases concerning such marriages arise today they are to be referred to the Holy Office. This would mean marriages contracted between non-Catholics and baptized Catholics either of non-Catholic parents or of a mixed marriage who had been raised outside of the Church since infancy, provided the marriage was contracted between 1908 and 1918.

In the Code, as has been said, express mention is made of these persons. While in the abstract the exemption of *ab acatholicis nati* is definite, the application of it to particular cases is often very difficult. It must be borne in mind that three conditions are necessary in order that the exemption of these persons who have been baptized be verified: (1) they must have non-Catholic parents, (2) be brought up from infancy in heresy, schism, infidelity, or without any religion, and (3) the exemption holds only for their marriage with a non-Catholic. Each condition must be present, the lack of one or the other will render the claim of exemption ineffective. In the following pages each condition will be examined in detail but at the same time it must always be remembered that the three conditions are inter-related.

First Condition: BORN OF NON-CATHOLICS. In recent years the Commission of Interpretation has given three decisions which have clarified the meaning of the elusive phrase *nati ab acatholicis*. There was never any doubt about it signifying children born of parents both of whom were non-Catholics. On July 20, 1929, the Commission declared that *ab acatholicis nati* embraced children of mixed and disparate marriages as well as children born of two non-Catholics.[61] A few months later, February 17, 1930, the same Commission stated that children of apostate parents were included in the meaning of "*ab acatholicis nati.*"[62] Later when asked about the force of the decision of July 20, 1929, the Commission declared that it was

[60] S. C. S. Off., 31 March, 1911—*A.A.S.*, III (1911), 163, 164.

[61] Pont. Comm. Interp. Cod., 20 July, 1929, ad II—*A. A. S.*, XXI (1929), 573.

[62] Pont. Comm. Interp. Cod., 17 February, 1930—*A. A. S.*, XXII (1930), 195.

declarative.[63] For the sake of clarity the import of these decisions will be considered under separate headings.

I. *"Ab acatholicis nati" include children of mixed and disparate marriages.*—This decision came as a surprise to the majority of canonists, who had taught the common opinion, namely, that *ab acatholicis nati* of canon 1099, § 2, meant children whose parents were both non-Catholic.[64] Two canonists, however, Leitner and Jone, took a different view. It was their opinion that the phrase *ab acatholicis nati* did not have to be restricted to those born of parents who were non-Catholics. They felt that there was some possibility of children of mixed or disparate marriage being included in its meaning. Of these the earlier was Leitner. He recalled the decree of the Holy Office of March 31, 1911, in which cases concerning *ab acatholicis nati* who had not observed the decree *Ne Temere* were to be referred to the Holy Office. In view of this Leitner believed that *ab acatholicis nati* may include children of mixed and disparate marriage. Therefore, he said such cases were to be sent to Rome even after the Code.[65]

Jone was of the opinion that the phrase *ab acatholicis nati* of canon 1099, § 2, gave rise to a doubt of law. Therefore, in virtue of canon 15, children of mixed and disparate marriages were exempted from the law. For a solution, however, a case would have to be sent to the Holy Office.[66] The Holy Office in a private reply to the Bishop of Limburg declared a marriage valid which had been contracted civilly between a non-Catholic girl and a man born of a mixed marriage, who had been baptized in the Catholic Church, but raised in heresy since infancy.[67] Before Jone had chance to publish this private answer which gave weight to his contention the Pontifical Commission gave its decision of July 20, 1929.

II. *"Ab acatholicis nati" includes children of apostates.*—In this

[63] Pont. Comm. Intertp. Codicis, July 25, 1931—*A. A. S.*, XXIII (1931), 388.

[64] Knecht, *Handbuch des katholischen Kirchenrechts*, p. 652; Wernz-Vidal, *Jus Canonicum*, V, n. 552 b; Cappello, *De Sacramentis*, III, n. 701; Linneborn, *Grundriss des Eherechts*, p. 381; Vermeersch-Creusen, *Epitome*, II, n. 407.

[65] *Lehrbuch des Katholischen Eherechts*, 3 ed., 1920, p. 210.

[66] *Theologisch-Praktische Quartalschrift*, LXXX (1927), 556-559.

[67] *Theologisch-Praktische Quartalschrift*, LXXXII (1929), 780, 781.

decision the Pontifical Commission speaks of the "children of apostates," not the apostates themselves. Apostates are always bound to the canonical form (canon 1099, § 1, n. 1). It must be kept in mind that such children are exempted provided: they have been brought up from infancy in heresy, etc., and marry a non-Catholic. These factors must always be considered. It seems admissible that if only one parent apostatizes—provided all other conditions are verified—a child will be exempt from the canonical form of marriage. The reason for this is the analogy which exists between the present decision of the Commission for Interpretation and the one given on July 20, 1929.[68]

In order to apply this decision one must know what persons constitute the class named "apostates." In the strict sense an apostate is a baptized person who has given up the Christian faith completely (canon 1325, § 2). In a broader use, canonists classify as apostates those who have left the Catholic Church and faith without becoming infidels.[69] If Catholics publicly become atheists, materialists, free thinkers and the like or if they formally embrace an heretical, or schismatic sect, or join a pagan cult, there will be little difficulty in classifying them as apostates. Gasparri notes that the decision of February 17, 1930, concerned public apostates.[70] Formal apostasy requires the ***intention*** of rejecting the faith, and the external manifestation of this intention.[71] Should all external indications point to a rejection of the faith but the intention be in doubt, one will be presumed an apostate in the external forum.[72] Negligence of parents in attendance at Mass and the sacraments and neglect of a child's religious education do not constitute apostasy. In practice it will be often difficult to say when parents have apostatized. As a rule, Catholic parents do not publicly reject the faith and very few formally ascribe themselves as converts to other religious sects. Neglect is a common failure frequently but neglect of duties is not necessarily rejection of beliefs. Hence, children of negligent Catholics are not

[68] *Periodica,* XX (1930), 77*-80*; *Apollinaris,* III (1930), 611, n. 12.
[69] *Periodica,* XIX (1930), 268-269; *A. E. R.,* LXXXIII (1930), 495.
[70] Gasparri, *De Matrimonio,* 4 ed., n. 1023.
[71] Cappello, *De Censuris,* n. 208.
[72] Cappello, *loc. cit.*

exempt from the canonical form of marriage. Cardinal Gasparri observes that the Holy Father may be asked to grant exemption to infants of Catholic parents who have been raised since infancy in heresy, schism, infidelity, or in no religion.[73] Under the decree *Tametsi* children in such conditions were classified as heretics and could enjoy the immunity of the Benedictine Declaration.[74]

If a child is born after his parents have apostatized he is truly *ab apostatis natus*.[75] What is the status of children whose parents have apostatized while they are infants, *i. e.*, at some period after they were born but before their use of reason? According to the letter of the law such children cannot be called *nati ab apostatis* and *per se*, even though reared outside the Catholic Church, they are subjects of the canonical form.[76] While this may be true, there is such a thing as equity in canon law and it would seem that canonical equity would supply a strong argument for the exemption of such children. From the time of the Benedictine Declaration the tendency of the Church has been more and more towards exempting from the canonical form those who have been in no way responsible for their subjection to it. Children who are born before their parents' apostasy and from infancy have been raised outside the Church are in the same condition as children whose birth followed the apostasy. It seems just to say that the law does not intend to exempt the latter and bind the former.

III. *The interpretation of July 20, 1929, was declarative:*—The decision which the Pontifical Commission gave on July 20, 1929, that *ab acatholicis nati* included children of mixed marriages was so opposed to the commonly received opinion that some asked if this interpretation were extensive or declarative. As has been mentioned the Commission replied that the interpretation which had been given was declarative.

The difference between an extensive and declarative interpretation lies principally in this: an extensive interpretation gives the words a broader sense or application than they really have while a merely

[73] *De Matrimonio*, 4 ed., n. 1029, in note.

[74] S. C. S. Off., 6 April, 1859—*Coll. P. F.*, n. 1174.

[75] *Apollinaris*, III (1930), 612.

[76] Maroto, *Apollinaris, loc. cit.*

declarative interpretation reaffirms a point of law that is clear in itself. An extensive interpretation is the equivalent of a new law and must be properly promulgated (canon 17, § 2). Since a declarative interpretation only reaffirms what is clear in itself, it requires no promulgation, and is retroactive in its effect. Applying these notions to the decision of July 20, 1929, it follows that the words *"ab acatholicis nati"* in themselves signify marriages in which either both parents are non-Catholics or only one is a non-Catholic; consequently children of mixed marriages have been exempted according to the special provisions of canon 1099, § 2, since the publication of the Code, Pentecost, 1918.[77]

In the latest edition of his treatise on Matrimony Cardinal Gasparri gives special consideration to the decision of the Commission which is now under discussion. He makes the general statement that the Pontifical Commission is only authorized to interpret the Code and cannot make new laws. He observes that the reply of 20 July, 1929, has no words, such as: *"facto verbo cum SSmo,"* etc., which would reveal that the content of the decision embodied a new law. He further points out that the Commission on another occasion interpreted the words in canon 987, *filii acatholicorum,* as including children of mixed marriages.[78] He next asks why children of mixed marriages who have been reared in heresy, etc., should not be included in the words *ab acatholicis nati.* Are they not in the same condition as children of two non-Catholic parents who have been reared in heresy, etc.? Finally, he states that the consultors who drafted the Code had in mind a reply of the Holy Office to the Bishop of Haarlem in Holland with reference to the meaning of heretics in the application of the exemption provided by the Benedictine Declaration.[79] In this reply of the Holy Office the term "heretic" was declared to include among other classes persons who had been baptized as Catholics but had been raised in heresy from infancy. This was a wide exemption. It prescinded from the concept of the religion professed by the parents and included even children of Catholic parents. The exemption of canon 1099, § 2, is not as broad as this. Cardinal Gasparri, in cit-

[77] *Cf.* Schaaf, *American Ecclesiastical Review,* LXXXIII (1930), 484-496.

[78] Pont. Comm. Int. Cod., 16 October, 1919; *A. A. S.,* XI (1919), 478.

[79] S. C. S. Off., 6 April, 1859—*Coll. P. F.,* n. 1174.

ing this former understanding of the term "heretic," wishes to demonstrate that the reply of the Commission in as far as it goes is in accord with the old law.[80]

It will be noticed that this decision stated that the reply of July 20, 1929, was declarative. What about the decision of February 17, 1930, regarding *filii ab apostatis?* Was that declarative or extensive? It must be admitted that the decision which stated that the Commission's reply was declarative only mentioned the decision of July 20, 1929. But *a pari* it would seem to apply to the decision concerning children of apostates. The Commission, according to Cardinal Gasparri, has no power to give extensive interpretations. The condition of children of apostates is surely the same, if not worse, as that of children of mixed marriage. Finally, it seems that no violence is done to the words *ab acatholicis nati* to read in them children of apostates for an apostate is a non-Catholic.[81] Canon 1325, § 2, gives the definition of heretic, apostate and schismatic; all three according to this canon have something in common, *i. e.*, they received Baptism. They differ in the manner of their rejection of Christianity. The difference, therefore, between these three is one of quantity (*plus et minus*). Heretics and schismatics are admittedly non-Catholics. Since apostates differ from them in degree alone it seems that an apostate may be correctly termed a non-Catholic. Moreover, observe that in paragraph three of canon 1325 Catholics are warned not to engage in controversy with non-Catholics. From the continuity of the canon it is natural to suppose that the term non-Catholic has been defined. This definition is given in paragraph two and includes heretics, schismatics and apostates.[82]

The conclusion seems to be warranted, therefore, that the decision of February 17, 1930, was merely declarative. It did no violence to the word *acatholicus* in including in it an apostate. It only reaffirms what was objectively clear.

[80] Gasparri, *De Matrimonio,* 4 ed., n. 1025-1029.

[81] Gasparri, *op. cit.*, n. 1023.

[82] *Jus Pontificium,* X (1930), 144.

Second Condition: BROUGHT UP FROM INFANCY IN HERESY, SCHISM, INFIDELITY OR IN NO RELIGION. The exemption afforded by canon 1099, § 2, requires as a second condition that those who are considered *ab acatholicis nati* must have grown up from infancy in heresy, schism, infidelity or without any religion. By infantile age (*aetas infantilis*) is understood the period prior to the acquisition of the use of reason. The law presumes that a child has acquired the use of reason when he has completed his seventh year.[83] It is to be noted, however, that the use of reason is only presumed. Presumption will cede to proven facts. Accordingly, if a *natus ab acatholicis* has been raised from infancy in some heretical or schismatical sect, or in a pagan cult, he will be exempted by canon 1099, § 2, from the form of marriage. Likewise, if he had no religious training and grew up from infancy in an entirely irreligious atmosphere, he will be exempted by the terms of the same canon. If, however, at any time after the seventh year, and previous to marriage a *natus ab acatholicis* were to receive a Catholic training or practice the Catholic religion, he *may be obliged* by the canonical form. The words "may be obliged" are italicized because the nature and amount of Catholic training as well as the length of practice of the Catholic religion are uncertain factors in every case. If they have been sufficient to cancel the second requiste of canon 1099, § 2—*i. e.*, render it impossible to say that he has been raised without any religion,—the exemption will cease; otherwise it will exist. Hence the question as to what amount of Catholic training, practice, and instruction is required to render the exemption of canon 1099, § 2, inapplicable?

This question is not easily answered. If a *natus ab acatholicis* has been raised from infancy in a heretical sect, or schismatical church, or is formally enrolled in a pagan cult, there does not seem to be any question of his exemption, even though incidentally he received some Catholic training. The reason for this lies in his formal adscription to these sects. The main difficulty centers, it

[83] Canon 88, § 3, "Impuberes, ante plenum septennium, dicitur infans seu puer vel parvulus, et censetur non sui compos; expleto autem septennio, usum rationis habere praesumitur."

seems, around persons of the class under discussion (*i e., ab acatholicis nati* of canon 1099, § 2), who have been raised without any religion or who have renounced their membership in some heretical sect and are practically without any religion; or again, those who, while professedly non-Catholics, are in reality non-believers. If such persons at any period between the age of seven and the time of marriage had a complete course or spent a few years in a Catholic school, thereby receiving the foundations at least of a Catholic education and training; or have received Confirmation; or frequented the Sacraments of Penance and the Holy Eucharist it seems certain that they are held by the canonical form of marriage. This training and practice would remove them from the class of exempt.[84]

The usual case which is presented to a Diocesan Tribunal does not contain patent evidences whereby it may easily be decided whether a *natus ab acatholicis* has received an education and training sufficient to bind him to the form of marriage. Frequently the cases regard marriage contracted without observing the form. The petitioner, having been divorced, is anxious to have a declaration of nullity due to the lack of form. The task usually presented to the Tribunal is to decide whether the Catholic education, training, etc., of the petitioner were sufficient to make him a subject of the canonical form. Frequently it happens that a Catholic relative secretly gave instructions to the petitioner, or he attended Sunday School for a period of months, or went to Mass, but never received the Sacraments; or he had undergone a course of instructions in preparation for reception into the Church, but was never received. The circumstances in these cases will vary greatly, and it is not too much to say that no two will be exactly alike. What course should a Diocesan Tribunal pursue? The Holy See has not given any criteria by which a Tribunal may judge a case of this kind. Hence, it seems that there is but one course to follow: provided that there is a reasonable doubt in the question of exemption or non-exemption from the canonical form, the case should be sent to the Holy Office for solution. In the preparation of the case all details which have any bearing on the amount of training and the home atmosphere of the petitioner should be minutely described; the nature of his Baptism

[84]Ayrhinac-Lydon, *Marriage Legislation*, p. 269.

and its circumstances; the character and habits of his parents, their religious outlook on life, and the practice of their duties should be also included. The more detailed the exposition of the case the better will the Holy Office be able to judge.[85]

Third Condition—THE FOREGOING ENJOY THIS EXEMPTION ONLY WHEN THEY MARRY NON-CATHOLICS.—The reason of this condition is the principle admitted in the decree *Ne Temere*,[86] and renewed in the Code that a person who is bound by the law of the canonical form is obliged to observe it even when marrying others who are exempt.[87] Hence, if persons of the exempted class wish to marry others who are held by the law, it will be necessary that the law be observed.

Canon 1099, § 2, states that *ab acatholicis nati* are exempt when they marry a non-Catholic party (*quoties cum parte acatholica contraxerint.*) Augustine takes these words as they sound and concludes that *ab acatholicis nati* are not exempt from the canonical form if they wish to marry others of their own class.[88] Other authors take a more lenient view and read the phrase "*quoties cum parte acatholica* . . . " to mean when they marry one who is exempt from the form. Hence since both *ab acatholicis nati* are exempt from the canonical form they may marry one another without observing it.[89] De Smet observes that the majority of writers follow this milder interpretation.[90] Payen believes this opinion probable but recognizes Augustine's as more probable. He recommends that the consent of these people be renewed in the canonical form *ad cautelam* should both become converts to the Church. In the event that one becomes a convert and wishes to marry some one else the case should be referred to the Holy Office because, in view of the opinion which considers such persons exempt from the canonical form, the marriage is not certainly invalid.[91]

[85] *Cf. Periodica,* XXI (1932), 14-16, in which an example is found of a case proposed to the Holy Office.

[86] Art. XI, § 2.

[87] Canon 1099, § 1, n. 2.

[88] Augustine, *Commentary,* V, p. 303, and Appendix II, p. 443.

[89] *A. E. R.*, LXXXIII (1930), 507, 508; *L'Ami du Clergé* (1924), 170, 171.

[90] *De Spons. et Matrimonio,* 4 ed., I, n. 143.

[91] Payen, *De Matrimonio,* II, n. 1843, in note.

CHAPTER VIII

THE EXTRAORDINARY FORM OF MARRIAGE

Canon 1098.—Si haberi vel adiri nequeat sine gravi incommodo parochus vel Ordinarius vel sacerdos delegatus qui matrimonio assistant ad normam canonum 1095, 1096:

1. In mortis periculo validum et licitum est matrimonium contractum coram solis testibus; et etiam extra mortis periculum, dummodo prudenter praevideatur eam rerum conditionem esse per mensem duraturam:

2. In utroque casu, si praesto sit alius sacerdos qui adesse possit, vocari et, una cum testibus, matrimonio assistere debet, salva coniugii validitate coram solis testibus.

THE Church is aware that under some circumstances it may be very difficult for people to contract marriage in the presence of her authorized witness in accordance with canon 1095 and 1096. To care for such situations the Code makes provision for the valid celebration of marriage before witnesses alone when the pastor, or Ordinary, or delegated priest cannot be had (*haberi vel adiri nequeat*) without serious inconvenience.[1] The Code permits marriage under

[1] The decree *Ne Temere* allowed for exceptions which resemble the provisions of canon 1098. It differed from the Code, however, in several ways. These differences will be noted in particular instances throughout this chapter. The decree *Tametsi* did not expressly mention any exceptions but the Sacred Congregations of the Council and the Propagation of the Faith in various replies and instructions sanctioned marriage before witnesses alone when it was impossible or very difficult to have an authorized priest. *Cf.* 30 March, 1669 —Benedict XIV, *De Synodo Dioecesana,* lib. XII, c. 5, n. 5; S. C. Prop., de Fide, 5 April, 1785—*Coll. P. F.,* n. 571; S. C. S. O., 1 July, 1863—*Coll. P. F.,* n. 1240; *Jus Pontificium,* VIII (1928), 174-182; IX (1929), 141-158.

these circumstances in two cases: (1) in danger of death; and (2) outside the danger of death, when it is prudently foreseen that the inability of having a priest to act as the qualified witness of the Church without serious inconvenience will last for a month (canon 1098, n. 1). In these cases the parties may validly marry in the presence of witnesses alone. If a priest should happen to be near at hand he should be called to assist together with the witnesses even though he has no authorization to act as the official witness of the Church. His presence, however, is not required for the validity of the marriage but only for its liceity. (Canon 1098, n. 2.)

The prescriptions of canon 1098 according to several authors constitute an extraordinary form of marriage.[2] Underlying the application of the extraordinary form of marriage is the serious inconvenience which is experienced in calling, or reaching a priest authorized to assist at marriage. With this as a foundation, canon 1098 lays down the requisites for the *valid* and *lawful* use of the extraordinary form of marriage. This chapter accordingly will be divided into two articles: the first, concerning the valid use of canon 1098; the second, its lawful use.

Article I. The Valid Use of Canon 1098.

In this article the nature of the grave inconvenience of having a competent priest for the marriage which is the basis of the use of the extraordinary form will first be examined; then, the application of this canon in danger of death and outside the danger of death.

1. *What constitutes a grave inconvenience?*

The valid use of the extraordinary form requires that the pastor or Ordinary or a delegated priest cannot without serious inconvenience be called or approached by the parties wishing to marry. If a priest may be had, who, although not delegated, can easily request delegation, it will be necessary to observe the ordinary form of marriage in his presence. Likewise, if the parties can conveniently go

[2] Aertnys-Damen, *Theologia Moralis*, II, n. 842; Payen, *De Matrimonio*, II, n. 1813; Vlaming, *Praelectiones Iuris Matrimonialis*, II, n. 584.

to another parish and be married there, the canon cannot be applied. The inconvenience must be felt in both calling the priest, and in going to him.[3] The Code requires that the inability of having or reaching a competent priest be personal. It does not mention any need of the cause coming from the physical condition of the locality in which the persons are dwelling. In this it differs from the decree *Ne Temere*,[4] which required that the inconvenience result from local conditions, (except in danger of death); it differs very probably also from the exceptions permitted under the decree *Tametsi*, which, according to some writers could be used only when the inability of having the priest was communal.[5] Under the present law, therefore, local inconvenience of having the competent witness, if it is not also personal, will not permit the use of canon 1098.[6] If the parties can conveniently approach a competent priest elsewhere they must do so. Even if the parties are the cause of the grave inconvenience—either by delaying the marriage, or by deliberately putting themselves in circumstances which make it seriously difficult to have or reach a competent priest—the privilege of canon 1098 may be invoked.[7]

It will be observed that canon 1098 does not require that the inability of having or reaching a competent priest be a physical impossibility, *e. g.*, at the risk of one's life. A *gravissimum incommodum* is not required. It is clear in exacting a *grave incommodum*.[8] In a case of a physical or moral impossibility of having a competent priest the Church recognizes the supremacy of the natural law giving man a right to marriage over the ecclesiastical law of the canonical form.[9] In such circumstances there would be no question of canon 1098, or

[3] Payen, *De Matrimonio,* II, n. 1816; Wouters, *De Forma . . . Celebrationis Matrimonii,* p. 38.

[4] S. C. C., decr., *Ne Temere,* 2 August, 1907, Art. VIII—*Fontes,* n. 4340.

[5] Gasparri, *De Matrimonio,* 3 ed., n. 1175; Wernz, *Jus Decretalium,* n. 173, note 165.

[6] Chelodi, *Ius Matrimonial,* n. 136, 137. Wouters, *op. cit.,* p. 38; Payen, *De Matrimonio,* II, n. 1816.

[7] S. C. de Sac., 12 March, 1910, ad. III—*A. A. S.,* II (1910), 195; Gasparri, *De Matrimonio,* 4 ed., n. 1008.

[8] Vromant, *Jus Missionariorum,* V, n. 203; Payen, *De Matrimonio,* n. 1817.

[9] Gasparri, *De Matrimonio,* 4 ed., n. 998.

of canons 1095, 1096. Marriage before witnesses alone would be valid. At times a marriage may be valid even if only one witness is available. In extreme circumstances (*e. g.*, if the parties could not otherwise marry, or would have to remain unmarried for a long time) a marriage without any witnesses would be valid.[10] Such circumstances will be very rare indeed yet are not impossible as Cardinal Gasparri observes.[11] Vromant observes that a marriage thus contracted by the use of *epikeia* ought to be made certainly valid either by a dispensation or a sanation.[12]

The inconvenience of having or approaching a priest competent to assist at the marriage may be due to a physical obstacle or even a moral one. The law requires that it be serious. The gravity will be judged by the individual and will vary with conditions of time, place, and other circumstances which may call for consideration in each case. Cardinal Gasparri indicates that no general norm can be set up by which the gravity of the particular inconvenience is to be judged. *"Incommodum enim quod mihi grave est tibi potest esse leve."*[13] The law is not to be considered tyrannical in its requirements. Much will depend upon circumstances and enlightened judgment. It is generally agreed that an inconvenience which is only *probably grave* will also admit the application of this canon.[14]

Owing to the innumerable varieties of circumstances which may combine to produce an inconvenience sufficiently serious to permit the application of the extraordinary form, it is impossible to classify and label all the instances of its use. Yet certain sources are recognized whence serious difficulty in having a competent priest may flow. External factors based upon natural causes, such as floods, storms, plagues, and excessive heat, may often (especially in danger of death),

[10] Gasparri, *loc. cit.;* Cappello, *De Sacramentis,* III, n. 695.

[11] He gives an example of a man dying in prison who wishes to contract a marriage which is civilly prohibited but is canonically lawful. It may happen that no witnesses can be present for fear of punishment by the civil law.—*Cf.* Gasparri, *op. cit.*, n. 998, 999.

[12] Vromant, *Jus Missionariorum,* V, n. 212; Van Hove, *De legibus ecclesiasticis,* n. 294.

[13] Gasparri, *De Matrimonio,* 4 ed., n. 1006.

[14] Wouters, *De Forma . . . Celebrationis Matrimonii,* p. 39; Payen, *De Matrimonio,* II, n. 1817.

give rise to a serious inconvenience of having a competent priest for the marriage. Likewise, conditions brought about by free causes, *e. g.*, persecutions, banditry, revolutions, may bring about a situation in which it will be difficult to observe the ordinary form of marriage.[15] An unsafe and difficult journey for either priest or parties may constitute a serious inconvenience.[16] At times a brief but arduous journey may constitute a serious inconvenience especially in mission districts and in the rural sections of this country. The nature of the emergency will of necessity have to be considered here. In the matter of distance alone a greater distance would be required, it would seem, than the distance which would exempt from hearing Mass. The ordinary means of communication only need be used in calling a priest to assist at the marriage or obtaining delegation to assist, *i. e.*, letter or messenger. The telegraph and telephone are still considered extraordinary means and if they were the only way by which the priest can be summoned or delegation obtained there would be no obligation to use them.[17] The aeroplane constitutes an extraordinary means of communication.[18] Some authors, *e. g.*, Cappello, consider the automobile and railroad as extraordinary means also. [19] Vlaming observes that the use of an auto in order to reach or call a priest can hardly be classified as a grave inconvenience today. Likewise he states that the use of the telegraph will scarcely involve a grave inconvenience.[20] Yet it is to be remembered that while the telegraph is highly developed, it is still a public medium of communication and liable to misuse. To this consideration is to be added the fact that not infrequently telegraphic messages because of their brevity and studied

[15] Gasparri, *De Matrimonio*, 4 ed., n. 1008; Vromant, *Jus Missionariorum*, V, n. 204; Payen, *De Matrimonio*, II, n. 1817.

[16] S. C. S. O., July, 1863—*Coll. P. F.*, n. 1240; S. C. de Sac., 12 March, 1910, ad III—*A. A. S.*, II (1910), 193.

[17] Payen, *De Matrimonio*, II, n. 1816; Wouters, *De Forma . . . Celebrationis Matrimonii*, p. 38; Vlaming, *Praelectiones Juris Matrimonialis*, II, n. 587; De Smet, *Betrothment and Marriage*, I, n. 131; Chelodi, *Jus Matrimoniale*, n. 136; Wernz-Vidal, *Jus Canonicum*, V, p. 641, note 63. *Cf.* also Pont. Comm. Interp. Cod., 12 November, 1922—*A. A. S.*, XIV (1922), 662, 663.

[18] Gasparri, *De Matrimonio*, 4 ed., n. 1008.

[19] Cappello, *De Sacramentis*, III, n. 491, 2; n. 236, 2.

[20] *Praelectiones Iuris Matrimonialis*, II, n. 587.

conciseness open the way to serious misunderstanding and confusion. A railroad trip of a few hours will hardly be a grave inconvenience, normally speaking.[21] In the theoretical consideration of these means of communication little can be said in general. The peculiar circumstances of the individual case and the nature of the emergency will supply more apt means of solution.

The poverty of the parties may in certain circumstances constitute the grave inconvenience spoken of in this canon when, for example, an expense relatively too great for them to undergo is necessary in order to reach a competent priest for the marriage.[22] The necessity of preserving the good name of an individual as well as the danger of violating the seal of confession may, at times, create an inconvenience in having a qualified witness for the marriage. Such inconvenience will permit the use of the extraordinary form of marriage. Thus, a confessor, according to many authors, may be released from the need of seeking delegation to assist at the marriage of a dying penitent who has revealed his condition of concubinage in confession. Likewise, there will be no necessity of the penitent to injure his good name by asking delegation for the confessor.[23] Although this opinion is expressed by several canonists of name, it may be asked whether it gives a reason which justifies the use of canon 1098. The preservation of the good name of the penitent *alone* in the case under consideration does not seem to justify a marriage before witnesses when the pastor may be called or delegation easily obtained. The reason seems too elastic and without foundation because the pastor is bound by his office to secrecy and he is to be trusted as much as the other witnesses which the use of canon 1098 require. Moreover, the good name of the parties may be well protected in a *matrimonium conscientiae* which is provided by law (canon 1104).

The competent priest may be hindered from assisting at the mar-

[21] Payen, *De Matrimonio,* II, n. 1817.

[22] Gasparri, *De Matrimonio,* 4 ed., n. 1998; *Cf.* instruction of the S. C. de P. F., 1785—*Coll. P. F.,* n. 571.

[23] Wouters, *De Forma . . . Celebrationis Matrimonii,* p. 38, in note; Wernz-Vidal, *Jus Canonicum,* V, n. 544; Cappello, *De Sacramentis,* III, n. 691; De Smet, *De Spons. et Matrimonio,* I, n. 131.

riage for various reasons, *e. g.*, illness, inclement weather, the external factors mentioned before, and also the fact that he cannot leave his mission because his presence is required for the common good of all.[24] In such instances he is physically absent from the place of the marriage. What is to be said of the case in which the pastor is present but is prohibited by the civil law under a severe penalty from assisting at the marriage. In certain States of this country there are laws against miscegenation, laws forbidding divorced persons from remarrying; or a law prohibiting the remarriage of a defendant in a divorce action. Not infrequently a penalty will be inflicted for the violation of these laws. It may happen, however, that persons of these classes in certain cases will be canonically free to marry. Can the pastor consider the penalty of the civil law an inconvenience sufficiently serious to permit the use of canon 1098?

The difficulty is not a new one for it was seriously debated under the decree *Ne Temere.*[25] The Sacred Congregation of the Sacraments, on the 31st of January, 1916, answered that in such cases (when the pastor could not assist because of the civil law) recourse should be made to the Holy See in each case except in danger of death when any priest could dispense from clandestinity and allow marriage before two witnesses alone.[26] Following the publication of the Code some authors believed that the physical absence of the pastor was necessary for the use of the canon 1098. In cases of fear of the civil law they believed that the instruction of 1916 continued in force and that the Holy See would have to be consulted in each case except in danger of death.[27] Other canonists believed that the reply of

[24] Payen, *De Matrimonio,* II, n. 1817; Gasparri, *De Matrimonio,* 4 ed., n. 1008.

[25] From various replies of the Sacred Congregations, it would seem that under the decree *Tametsi,* not only the physical absence of the pastor was required for a marriage before witnesses but also a moral absence sufficed. Here, fear of punishment might be so construed as to constitute the priest morally absent. *Cf.* S. C. S. O., 1 July, 1863, *ad Episc. Valisprat—Coll. P. F.,* n. 1240; also S. C. P. F., 1785, *ad Praefectum Missionum in Insula Curacao—Coll. P. F.,* n. 571.

[26] S. C. de Sacramentis—*A. A. S.,* VIII (1916), 36.

[27] Linneborn, *Grundriss des Eherechts nach dem Codex I. C.* (Paderborn, 1919), p. 372, 415; Wernz-Vidal, *Jus Canonicum,* V, n. 547; Oesterle, *Jus Pontificium,* VIII (1928), 174-182; IX (1929), 141-158.

the Sacred Congregation of January 31, 1916, had been abrogated by the code and consequently taught that marriage could be celebrated in the presence of witnesses alone if the competent priest was prohibited from assisting because of fear of a civil punishment.[28]

After the Code a doubt concerning the absence of the priest as required by canon 1098 was again proposed to the Congregation of the Sacraments which referred it to the Commission of Interpretation.[29] It was framed thus: "Is canon 1098 to be understood in the sense that it refers only to the physical absence of the Ordinary or parish priest?" The answer dated March 10, 1928, was *affirmative*.[30] This decision seemed to end all doubt and take the matter out of the realm of controversy. Canonists at once taught that the obstacles to the pastor's presence had to be of a physical character, such as sickness, bad roads, snow, etc. They held that moral absence, namely, inability to assist because of a prohibitive civil law, would not permit the use of canon 1098.[31] It is to be noted that in requiring the *physical absence* of the pastor this decision excludes the use of canon 1098 in other circumstances in which the pastor might be said to be morally absent, *e. g.*, when of his own accord he refuses to assist at a mixed marriage either because he hopes to prevent the marriage by his refusal, or because he doubts the sincerity of the promises made by the non-Catholic party.

On July 25, 1931, another decision was published by the Commission of Interpretation. It was given in answer to a doubt concerning the decision of March 10, 1928: "Is the physical absence of the parish priest or Ordinary, which was spoken of in the interpretation given on March 10, 1928, concerning canon 1098, verified in a case in which the parish priest or Ordinary cannot assist at the celebration of a marriage because of a serious inconvenience, asking and receiving the consent of the parties, although they (the pastor or

[28] Vlaming, *Praelectiones Juris Matrimonialis,* 11, n. 590; Chelodi, *Jus Matrimoniale,* n. 136; Cappello, *De Sacramentis,* II, n. 694; Vermeersch-Creusen, *Epitome,* II, n. 405.

[29] Gasparri, *De Matrimonio,* 4 ed., n. 1016.

[30] *A. A. S.,* XX (1928), 120.

[31] Vromant, *Jus Missionariorum,* V, n. 203; Maroto, *Apollinaris,* I (1928), 334-339; Vermeersch, *Periodica,* XVII (1928), 76.

Ordinary) are materially present in the place." The answer was *affirmative*.[32]

In the latest revision of his treatise on Marriage, Cardinal Gasparri explicitly states that the inconvenience which the Commission had in mind when giving the decision of July 25, 1931, was the inconvenience caused by a civil law which forbade a priest to assist at a marriage which otherwise could be canonically contracted.[33] Some commentators had understood the reply in this sense; [34] others, however, declared it was only a wider interpretation of physical absence. They still maintained that the inability of the pastor to assist, even though he was materially present, had to be the result of a physical impediment, *e. g.*, loss of mind, fear of contagious disease and the like. They did not see in the reply the admission of fear of civil punishment as a *ratio sufficiens* for the use of canon 1098.[35] Following the explicit revelation of the mind of the Commission of Interpretation, as made by its President, Cardinal Gasparri, there need be no further doubt as to whether fear of punishment by the civil law will suffice to permit the use of canon 1098. If a competent priest cannot be otherwise approached, (*e. g.*, by going into another State and being married by a priest there who is not hindered by civil law from assisting), then in danger of death, fear of a serious fine or sentence to prison will excuse a priest from assisting and the marriage may be celebrated before witnesses alone. Outside the danger of death this may be done if it is prudently foreseen that the inability to assist will continue for a month.[36]

What is to be said, however, concerning the decision of the Pontifical Commission of March 10, 1928, as contrasted with the one of July 25, 1931? At least there seems to be an apparent conflict for the former declared that physical absence of the pastor was necessary for the use of canon 1098; the latter recognized the use of canon

[32] *A. A. S.*, XXIII (1931), 388.

[33] Gasparri, *De Matrimonio*, 4 ed., n. 1017.

[34] *American Ecclesiastical Review*, LXXXV (1931), 635; *Periodica*, XXI (1932), 43-45.

[35] Maroto, *Apollinaris*, IV (1931), 381, 382; *Jus Pontificium*, XI (1931), 255; *Ephemerides Theologicae Lovanienses*, IX (1932), 284-291; *Homiletic Review* (1931), 191.

[36] Gasparri, *De Matrimonio*, 4 ed., 1017.

1098 in circumstances in which the pastor was physically present but could be said to be morally absent.

Gasparri takes cognizance of this apparent conflict, and mentions that the decision of March 10, 1928, is to be understood in the sense that moral presence of the priest at marriage is not sufficient; he must be physically present and ask and receive the consent of the parties.[87] Yet when one rereads the decision of March 10, 1928, in the light of Gasparri's observation its meaning is still obscure. The *dubium* as proposed gives no hint that the point at issue was the moral presence of the pastor and his refusal to ask and receive the consent of the parties.[88] From Gasparri's revelation, however, the Commission must have such cases in mind, for example, when the pastor, while present in person, refused of his own volition to assist at a mixed marriage because he wished to prevent the marriage by his refusal or because he felt that in conscience he could not assist as he doubted the sincerity of the promises made by the non-Catholic party. In these circumstances a doubt might arise whether such a pastor could be considered "absent" (*haberi vel adiri nequit*) in the sense of canon 1098. It would seem from Gasparri's explanation that such "absence" was what the Commission discussed in its decision of March 10, 1928, and it declared that in those circumstances a marriage would be invalid unless the pastor assisted at the marriage actively by asking and receiving the consent of parties as directed by canon 1095, § 1, n. 3.

Another obscurity remains. The reply of 1928 in its generality excluded the use of canon 1098 when the pastor was impeded from assisting because he feared punishment at the hands of the civil law. From the general tenor of the decision it must be admitted that this is so. Yet there is no proof that the Commission had this particular case in mind. On the other hand, there is the decision of the Con-

[87] "Responsio igitur data die 10 martii, 1928, ita est intelligenda, ut ad matrimonii valorem non sufficiat praesentia moralis, sed sit necessaria praesentia physica et activa, ita scilicet ut sacerdos assistens nupturientium consensum exquirat et recipiat ad normam rel., canon 1095, § 1, n. 3"—Gasparri, *De Matrimonio*, 4 ed., n. 1017.

[88] "An canon 1098 ita intelligendus sit ut referatur tantum ad physicam parochi vel Ordinarii absentiam? Resp. Affirmative."—*Pont. Comm. Interp. Cod.—A. A. S.*, XX (1928), 120.

gregation of the Sacraments in 1916 which laid down the rule for this case. It could have been that the Commission in its reply of 1928 did not consider this case of fear arising from a prohibition of the civil law believing that such circumstances were already cared for by the instruction of the Congregation of the Sacraments already mentioned. Most commentators, however, understood the decision of March 10, 1928, to refer to this particular case of the inability of a priest to assist because he feared punishment from the civil law.[39] In the decision, however, of July 25, 1931, according to Cardinal Gasparri, the Commission had particularly in mind the inconvenience which was caused by fear of the civil law.[40] If there is to be any harmonizing between the two decisions, it seems that it must rest on the grounds that they contemplated different cases. The decision of March 10, 1928, considered the instances in which the pastor of his own accord refused to assist as has been explained above while the decision of July 25, 1931, concerned the much discussed moral absence caused by fear of punishment by civil law. Much of the misunderstanding may have been avoided, however, if the *dubium* of March 10, 1928, had been framed in a manner which would have revealed the particular circumstances to which it referred.

2. *The Cases in Which Canon 1098 May Be Applied.*

The law contemplates two cases in which it may be necessary to use the extraordinary form of marriage, namely, in danger of death and outside such a danger when it is prudently foreseen that the inability of calling or approaching a competent priest will last for a month.

A. In Danger of Death. No other condition is necessary for the valid use of this canon when there is danger of death to either of the parties other than the inability of having a competent priest with-

[39] *Jus Pontificium*, VIII (1928), 5, 6; *Apollinaris*, I (1928), 334-339; *Monitore Ecclesiastico*, 4 series, X (1928), 106.

[40] "Grave autem incommodum quod pontificia Commissio in hac responsione prae oculis praesertim habuit, erat incommodum proveniens a civili lege, matrimonium sub gravibus poenis vetante"—Gasparri, *De Matrimonio*, 4 ed., n. 1017.

out a serious inconvenience. This inconvenience will be judged in the light of the preceding section of this article. Canon 1098 does not require imminent death as the decree *Ne Temere*.[41] It speaks of danger of death. Death need not be certain, or even proximate, but there must be a reasonable danger that any delay may prevent the marriage either through the death of one of the persons or render it impossible because of the delirious condition of the patient.[42]

Under the decree *Ne Temere* a motivating cause was required to permit marriage without the priest in danger of death.[43] According to Cardinal Gasparri this requirement of the *Ne Temere* decree was purposely omitted in the Code.[44] Hence, under the Code the only requirement in this regard is that there be danger of death. The cause from which death may follow may be intrinsic, *e. g.*, sickness, or difficult delivery, etc.; or it may be extrinsic, as a storm, earthquake, a sentence of capital punishment, impending battle, and the like.[45] The seriousness and probability of death will have to be judged by the circumstances of the particular case. Once a judgment has been made to the best of one's ability there need be no scruple. Should the danger pass away shortly after the marriage has been celebrated or should it be learned later that a priest could have been called in time, there need be no anxiety concerning the validity of the marriage. An error in judgment will not invalidate the use of the canon unless the error was altogether absurd.[46] The legislator does not demand accuracy, but only expects a prudent and enlightened judgment made according to the capacity of the individual and the circumstances of the case.[47]

B. OUTSIDE DANGER OF DEATH. In canon 1098 the use of the

[41] S. C. C., decr., *Ne Temere*, 2 August, 1907, Art. VII—*Fontes*, n. 4340.

[42] Vromant, *Jus Missionariorum*, V, n. 202.

[43] " . . . ad consulendum conscientiae et (si casus ferat) legitimationi prolis . . ."—S. C. C. decret., *Ne Temere*, 2 August, 1907, Art. VII—*Fontes*, n. 4340.

[44] Gasparri, *op. cit.*, n. 1007.

[45] Gasparri, *loc. cit.*

[46] Gasparri, *loc. cit.;* Vromant, *Ius Missionariorum*, V, n. 202; Cappello, *De Sacramentis*, III, n. 691; Payen, *De Matrimonio*, II, n. 1815.

[47] Wernz-Vidal, *Ius Canonicum*, V, n. 544; Chelodi, *Ius Matrimoniale*, n. 136; Cappello, *loc. cit.*

extraordinary form of marriage is not limited alone to the emergency caused by danger of death. The law contemplates another case in which it may be used, namely, outside danger of death, when a competent priest cannot be had without grave inconvenience and *it is prudently foreseen that this state of affairs will continue for a month.* The decree *Ne Temere* had required that the competent witness be actually absent for a month before marriage in the presence of witnesses alone was allowed.[48] The Code only requires that the inability of having the competent witness be prudently *foreseen* to last a month. This inconvenience may be based either upon a physical obstacle, *e. g.*, weather, sickness and the like; or it may arise from the prohibition of the civil law which restrains the competent witness under penalty from assisting at a marriage. The inconvenience must be personal and need not of necessity result from local conditions. On the other hand a local inconvenience will not suffice if it is not at the same time personal.[49] The gravity of the inconvenience and its duration will be decided by prudent judgment. The marriage will be valid even if the priest returns or is in a position to assist within a month, provided, at the time of the celebration, his return had not been prudently foreseen.[50] If the parties can conveniently go to a competent priest elsewhere they are obliged to do so.[51] The use of this canon will be valid even if the parties deliberately went to a place in which they foresaw that a priest could not be had without serious inconvenience;[52] or if they delayed their marriage until the situation was such that a priest could not be had for a month.[53]

This second case as contemplated in canon 1098 is more likely to occur in missionary districts. Yet it may be realized also in this country, as for example, if a State law were to forbid marriage be-

[48] S. C. C. decret., "*Ne Temere*," 2 August, 1907, Art. VIII—*Fontes*, n. 4340.

[49] S. C. de Sacramentis, 12 March, 1910, ad I, II—*Fontes*, n. 2101; S. C. C., 27 July, 1908, ad V—*A. A. S.*, LXI (1908), 511; Chelodi, *Jus Matrimoniale*, n. 137.

[50] Gasparri, *De Matrimonio*, 4 ed., n. 1009.

[51] De Smet, *De Spons. et Matrimonio*, I, n. 131.

[52] S. C. de Sacramentis, 13 March, 1910, ad III—*A. A. S.*, II (1910), 193.

[53] Payen, *De Matrimonio*, II, n. 1918, note 2; Gasparri, *De Matrimonio*, 4 ed., n. 1008.

tween persons otherwise canonically free to marry. In some States both parties to a divorce are not permitted to remarry. It may happen that a Catholic has contracted a civil marriage and later obtained a divorce and now wishes to marry. If granted a declaration of nullity in an Ecclesiastical Tribunal, he would be free to marry but hindered by the particular law of such a State. What is to be done if he cannot afford to travel to an adjoining State where he may legally marry? In such a case, a marriage before witnesses would be valid, provided it were prudently foreseen that the inability of being married before a competent witness would continue for a month.[54] Great caution and care will have to be exercised in the application of this particular phase of canon 1098 but once the circumstances are such as permit its use there need be no fear of the validity of the marriage.

The month's duration should be complete and calculated from the day of the marriage. It should not be reckoned for example from the 2nd of March and the marriage took place on the 10th of March. If it is prudently foreseen that the priest will return within a month's time, a marriage would be invalid if contracted before witnesses alone.[55] The computation of the month will follow the norm of canon 33, § 3. It is to be taken according to the calendar, *e. g.*, from March 2nd to April 2nd. If the reckoning of the month coincides with the beginning of the day, *i. e.*, on midnight on March 1st, it will end on midnight of April 1st (canon 33, § 3, n. 2). This will rarely occur. If the reckoning starts sometime during the day of March 2nd the month will not be complete until midnight of April 2nd (canon 33, § 3, n. 3). In the event that the computation began on January 31st, the month is considered complete on midnight of February 28th or 29th (canon 33, § 3, n. 4).

It has been said that it must be prudently judged that the inability of having a competent witness will continue for a month. The Pontifical Commission of Interpretation has declared that this judgment is to be based upon a moral certitude resulting from an investigation on the part of the persons, or from public and notorious infor-

[54] Gasparri, *De Matrimonio,* 4 ed., n. 1017.

[55] Gasparri, *De Matrimonio,* 4 ed., n. 1009.

mation, *e. g.*, from letters, or a custom known to all that the priest leaves every year at a certain season. Hence, the fact that a priest is not present does not suffice to use canon 1098. An inquiry must be made concerning his absence and the duration of his absence. Only after the parties are morally certain that he will be gone for a month may the privilege of the canon be used.[56] The investigation spoken of is required before the marriage. What is to be said of a marriage which has been already contracted without the priest and no investigation had been made? The case may become practical for certain mountainous or rural parts of this country. The case can easily be supposed in which a Catholic in such a locality marries a non-Catholic before a civil officer. No previous investigation was made about a Catholic priest nor was any attempt made to reach him. Are these persons validly married? Before attempting to consider this problem it will be well to state that the valid use of canon 1098 does not require that the parties realize or be conscious of the exemption which the canon provides. Given, on the one hand, that they sincerely wish to contract marriage, and on the other, that the conditions of the canon are present (*i. e.*, they cannot get the priest and death is feared; or they know that he will not return for several months) the marriage will be valid; *de facto* they are within the law. Nowhere in canon 1098 is it stated that knowledge of the exception to the general law is necessary. Even if the parties were to believe erroneously that a priest was required for their marriage (while *de facto* because of circumstances, he was not) they would marry validly before witnesses provided true matrimonial consent was given and there were no diriment impediments. Thus for example, two persons in the Oceanic Island would marry validly, if, knowing that the missionary would not come for months, they went before a civil officer to be married erroneously thinking, however, that they were obliged to await the priest. Such a marriage is valid in virtue of canon 1098 and there is no need of a second religious ceremony. In going through the civil marriage, the requisites of the extraordinary form were observed, *i. e.*, a marriage before witnesses alone.[57]

[56] Pont. Com. Interp. Cod., November 10, 1925, ad VIII—*A. A. S.*, XVII (1925), 583.

[57] Payen, *De Matrimonio*, II, n. 1819, in note 1, p. 222; *L'Ami du Clergé*

What is to be said, however, of the case in which no investigation preceded, when the priest was ignored and marriage contracted civilly, and it developed later that the priest was actually absent for a month? Such a marriage will not necessarily be invalid. An investigation will have to be made in order to learn whether the absence of the priest for a month could have been prudently foreseen. If the result shows that the priest could not have been conveniently summoned; or that the parties could not have approached him without serious inconvenience and all of this could have prudently been foreseen,— the marriage will be valid. Canon 1098 does not imply that for its valid use the parties personally must be aware of the month's absence. It seems sufficient that the state of affairs in the place warrant this conclusion, if they had been examined.[58] If on the other hand investigation reveals that a priest could have been called, or was present, or returned within the month, or could have easily been approached, the marriage will be invalid. In event that no positive results are obtained from subsequent investigation, the marriage will be invalid.[59] These facts may be of practical consideration in certain petitions of nullity on the grounds that the canonical form was neglected.

3. *Canon 1098 Requires the Presence of Witnesses.*

The valid use of canon 1098, whether in danger of death or outside it, requires the presence of *at least* two witnesses. This is evident from the wording of the canon *contractum coram testibus.* The presence of witnesses are required for validity. It should be carefully noted that in the application of canon 1098, two witnesses must always be used. Earlier in this article it was said that if circum-

5 series, n. 37 (1933), 587. *Cf.* also canon 1085; *Cf.* also Payen, *De Matrimonio,* II, Casus 259, p. 232.

[58] The reply of the Pontifical Commission does not seem to contemplate the case mentioned; it simply stated that mere absence alone of the priest will not suffice for the application of canon 1098. In the case under consideration, the facts are: The people married before witnesses and objectively the priest could not have been had for a month because of local conditions and *had an investigation been made this would have been known.*

[59] Vermeersch, *Periodica,* XIV (1925), 185, 186.

stances were so extreme as to render it impossible to have two witnesses one would suffice. In extraordinary circumstances if no witnesses were available marriage could be validly celebrated without them. In such cases a marriage is valid because the natural right of man to marry will prevail over the ecclesiastical law which prescribe the canonical form; in such circumstances its validity does not arise from the use of canon 1098.[60]

As in the use of the ordinary form no mention was made of specific qualities in the witnesses, so also in the extraordinary form. There is no obligation for them to ask the consent of the parties or to receive it. They are required to perceive the exchange of matrimonial consent in such a manner as to be able to testify to it whenever such testimony be necessary.[61] Following the marriage the witnesses are obliged under a serious obligation to see to the proper recording of it as soon as possible.[62]

Article II. The Lawful Use of Canon 1098

In the second part of canon 1098 the law prescribes that if another priest is at hand who may be present for the marriage (either in danger of death, or not) he should assist at the marriage with the other witnesses. The priest must be at hand (*praesto*); the parties need not search for him.[63] The canon adds immediately, however, that *his presence is not required for the validity of the marriage.*[64] The priest spoken of in this canon is one who otherwise is not qualified to assist at the marriage as he is neither pastor nor Ordinary nor delegate of either. In assisting he acts as a *special witness,* not as the *testis auctorizabilis.* This is evident from the fact that his presence is not required for the validity of the marriage. He need not interrogate the parties, nor receive the expression of their consent; yet this

60 Vromant, *Jus Missionariorum,* V, n. 205; Wouters, *De Forma . . . Celebrationis Matrimonii,* p. 42.

61 S. C. P. F., 23 June, 1830—*Coll. P. F.,* n. 816.

62 Canon 1103; Gasparri, *De Matrimonio,* 4 ed., n. 1013.

63 Augustine, *Commentary,* V, p. 295.

64 In the decree *Ne Temere,* the presence of the priest was necessary in danger of death. *Cf.* S. C. C. decret., *Ne Temere,* 2 August, 1907, Art. VII—*Fontes,* n. 4340; De Smet, *De Spons. et Matrimonio,* I, 133, in note 2.

is not forbidden him.[65] The obligation of calling the priest would certainly cease in the event that so doing would involve a serious inconvenience; [66] Cappello even believes that a just cause would excuse from this obligation.[67] Must a priest be called if he is under a censure? If no sentence has been passed upon him declaring or inflicting the censure, Cappello states that a censured priest must be summoned to assist at the marriage.[68] Cerato holds that a *vitandus* or a *toleratus post sententiam* must be called to assist at the marriage if he is available and no other priest is present. The majority of writers, however, take the view that there is no obligation resting upon the parties to call such a priest.[69] However, in danger of death, the parties *may* lawfully call a *vitandus* or *toleratus post sententiam* in order to bless the marriage, as well as to administer the other sacramentals that have place in the Catholic celebration of marriage (canon 2261, § 3). Outside danger of death it does not seem that a *vitandus* or *toleratus post sententiam* may be lawfully asked to assist at the marriage.[70]

The Church requires the presence of a priest at the extraordinary form of marriage in order to insure its valid celebration, to add a religious atmosphere, and to guarantee its proper registration. The priest assisting in the manner directed by canon 1098 enjoys faculties to dispense in many impediments when there is danger of death. Outside danger of death he may dispense in occult cases if everything is prepared for the marriage.[71] It is evident that his presence aids in the religious celebration of the marriage, and stresses its sacred character. In placing upon him an obligation, serious indeed, of recording the marriage and as soon as possible the parties will be

[65] Wouters, *De Forma . . . Celebrationis Matrimonis*, p. 42; Wernz-Vidal, *Jus Canonicum*, V, n. 543; Gasparri, *De Matrimonio*, 4 ed., n. 1101; Vromant, *Jus Missionariorum*, V, n. 210; De Smet, *De Spons. et Matrimonio*, I, n. 133.

[66] Wernz-Vidal, *loc. cit.*

[67] *De Sacramentis*, III, n. 696.

[68] *Loc. cit.*

[69] De Smet, *De Spons. et Matrimonio*, I, p. 138, note 1; Capello, *loc. cit.;* Vlaming, *Praelectiones Iuris Matrimonialis*, II, n. 586.

[70] Hyland, E., *Excommunication*, pp. 107-109.

[71] Canon 1044 compared with 1043; also canon 1045, § 3; Cappello, *De Sacramentis*, III, n. 696.

better assured of its proper registration.[72] Moreover, while the priest who assists in the manner directed by this canon is not the *testis auctorizabilis* of the Church, he may be otherwise qualified by the civil law to perform marriages. His presence at the extraordinary form of marriage will therefore remove possible inconvenience which could arise from certain requirements of the civil law.

[72] Canon 1103.

BIBLIOGRAPHY

Sources

Acta Sanctae Sedis, 41 vols., Rome, 1865-1908.

Acta Apostolicae Sedis, Typis Polygottis Vaticanis, 1909.

Acta et Decreta Conciliorum Recentiorum (Collectio Lacensis), 7 vols., Freiburg in Breisgau, 1870-1890.

Berardi, C., *Gratiani Canones Genuini ab Apocryphis Discreti, Corrupti ad emendationem Codicum Fidem Exacti, Difficiliores Commoda interpretatione illustrati,* 4 vols., Venice, 1777.

Bullarium SSmi Domini Nostri Benedicti Papae XIV, 4 vols., 4 ed., Venice, 1778.

Bullarii Romani Continuatio Summorum Pontificum, 19 vols., Prato, 1756-1883.

Codex Iuris Canonici, Rome, 1918.

Codicis Iuris Canonici Fontes, cura Emi. Petri Card. Gasparri editi, 6 vols., Rome, 1923-1933.

Collectanea S. Congregationis de Propaganda Fide, 2 vols., Rome, ex Typographia Polygotta, 1907.

Concilium Plenarium Baltimori Habitum Anno 1852, Baltimore, 1853.

Concilii Plenarii Baltimorensis, II, Acta et Decreta, Baltimore, 1868.

Concilii Plenarii Baltimorensis, III, Acta et Decreta, Baltimore, 1886.

Concilii Tridentini Diariorum, Actorum Epistolarum, Tractatuum Nova Collectio, edidit Societas Goerresiana, 8 vols., Freiburg, 1901-1919.

Corpus Iuris Canonici (Richter-Freidberg), 2 vols., Leipzig-Welter, 1922.

Corpus Iuris Civilis (Krueger-Mommsen-Schoell-Kroell), 5 ed., 3 vols., Berlin, Weidman, 1928.

Mansi, J., *Sacrorum Conciliorum Nova et Amplissima Collectio,* 53 vols., Paris-Arnheim-Leipzig, 1901-1927.

Migne, J., *Patrologiae Cursus Completus*—Series Latina, 221 vols., (MPL), Paris, 1844-1855; Series Graeca, 161 vols. (MPG) Paris, 1858-1864.

Pallotini, Salvator, *Collectio Omnium Conclusionum et Resolutionum quae in causis propositis apud S. Cong. Cardinalium S. Concilii Tridentini Interpretum prodierunt ab anno 1564 ad annum 1860,* 17 vols., Rome, 1868-1893.

Rituale Romanum, Auctoritate SSmi D. N. Pii Papae XI ad Normam C. I. C. Accomodatum, 2 ed., Ratisbonae, 1926.

Richter-Schulte, *Canones et Decreta Concilii Tridentini,* Leipzig, 1853.

S. Romanae Rotae Decisiones seu Sententiae, Rome, 1909.

Theodosiani Libri XVI cum Constitutionibus Sirmondianis (Kreuger-Mommsen edition), 3 vols., Berlin, 1895.

Reference Works

Aertnys-Damen, *Theologia Moralis,* 11 ed., 2 vols., Turin, Marietti, 1928.

Aquinas, St. Thomas, *Opera Omnia,* ed., Frette, Paris, 1873-1879.

Alzog, *Manual of Church History,* 4 vols., ed., nova., Gill and Sons, Dublin, 1874.

Artaud, Le Chevalier, *Histoire du Pape Pius VII,* 2 vols., Paris, 1837.

Augustinus, Antonius, *Antiquae Collectiones Decretalium,* Lerida, 1576.

Ayrinhac-Lydon, *Marriage Legislation in the New Code of Canon Law,* New York, Benziger, 1932.

[Bachofen], Charles Augustine, *A Commentary on the New Code of Canon Law,* 4 ed., 8 vols., St. Louis, Herder, 1921-1929.

Baronius, Caesarius Cardinal, *Annales Ecclesiastici,* 37 vols., Bari, 1864-1883.

Benedict XIV, *De Synodo Diocesana,* 2 vols., Rome, Typographia S. C. de P. F., 1806.

Bingham, Joseph, *The Antiquities of the Christian Church,* 9 vols., London, 1844.

Blat, A., *Commentarium Textus Codicis Iuris Canonici,* 6 vols., Rome, Ex Typographia in Instituto Pii IX, 1921-1927.

Bory, P., *Un commento al canone di somma importanza concernente la celebrazione del Matrimonio cattolico,* Malta, 1924.

Boudinhom, A., *Le Mariage et Les Fiancailles,* 4 ed., Lethielleux, Paris, 1907.

Cance, A., *Le Code de Droit Canonique,* 6 ed., 3 vols., Paris, 1930.

Cappello, F., *Tractatus Canonico-Moralis de Sacramentis,* 2 ed., 3 vols., Vol. III, *De Matrimonio,* Rome, Marietti, 1927.

——— *De Censuris,* 2 ed., Rome, Marietti, 1925.

Catholic Encyclopedia, 17 vols., New York, The Encyclopedia Press, 1907-1922.

Cerato, *Matrimonium a Codice Iuris Canonici Integre Desumptum,* 4 ed., Padua, Typis Seminar., 1929.

Chelodi, J., *Ius Matrimoniale iuxta Codicem Iuris Canonici,* 3 ed., Trent, Libr. Edit. Trident., 1921.

——— *Ius de Personis iuxta Codicem Iuris Canonici,* 2 ed., Trent, Libr. Edid. Trident., 1927.

Cocchi, *Commentarium in Codicem Iuris Canonici,* 7 vols., Turin, 1925-1927.

Corbett, Percy, *Roman Law on Marriage,* Oxford, Clarendon Press, 1930.

Coronata, M., *Institutiones Iuris Canonici,* vol. I, Turin, 1928.

Costello, J., *Domicile and Quasi-Domicile,* Washington, Catholic University, 1930.

Creagh, J., *A Commentary on the Decree Ne Temere,* Baltimore, Furst, 1908.

Cronin, *The New Matrimonial Legislation,* New York, Benziger, 1908.

D'Annibale, J., *Summula Theologiae Moralis,* 3 ed., 3 vols., Rome, 1892.

DeBecker, Julius, *Legislatio Nova de Forma Substantiali quoad Sponsalia et Matrimonia Catholicorum,* 3 ed., Louvain, 1913.

——— *Praelectiones Canonicae De Matrimonio,* ed., nova., Louvain, 1931.

DeMeester, A., *Iuris Canonici et Iuris canonico-Civilis Compendium,* 3 vols., Bruges, 1921-1928.

DeSmet, A., *De Sponsalibus et Matrimonio,* 4 ed., Bruges, Beyaert, 1927.

Duschene, L., *Christian Worship: Its Origin and Evolution,* London, 1903.

Duskie, J., *Canonical Status of Orientals in the United States,* Washington, Catholic University, 1928.

Esmein, A., *Le Mariage en Droit Canonique,* 2 ed., revised by R. Genestal, vol. I, Paris, Libraire du Recueil Sirey, 1929.

Fanfani, L., *De Iure Parchorum ad Normam Codicis Iuris Canonici,* Turin, Marietti, 1924.

Farrugia, P. N., *De Matrimonio et Causis Matrimonialibus, tractatus canonico-moralis iuxta Codicem Iuris Canonici,* Rome, 1924.

Feiji, H., *De Impedimentis et Dispensationibus Matrimonialibus,* 3 ed., Louvain, 1885.

Ferry, W., *Stole Fees,* Washington, Catholic University, 1930.

Fleiner, Fritz, *Die Tridentinische Ehevorschrift,* Leipzig, H. Haessel, 1892.

Fourneret, Pierre, *Le Mariage Chretien,* Paris, Beauchesne, 1925.

Freisen, J., *Geschichte des Canonischen Eherechts,* Paderborn, 1893.

Friedberg, E., *Das Recht der Eheschliessung,* Leipzig, Tauchnitz, 1865.

Gally, H., *Considerations on Clandestine Marriages,* 2 ed., London, 1750.

Gasparri, Petrus, *Tractatus Canonicus de Matrimonio,* 3 ed., 2 vols., Paris, Beauchesne, 1904.

——— *Tractatus Canonicus de Matrimonio,* ed. nova ad mentem Codicis Iuris Canonici, Rome, Typis Polygottis Vaticanis, 1932.

Gennari, Casmiro, *Breve Commento della nuova Legge sugli Sponsali e sul Matrimonio,* 4 ed., Rome, Monitore Ecclesiastico, 1908.

Giraldi, Ubaldus, *Expositio Iuris Pontificii,* 2 vols., Rome, 1830.

Gothofredus, J., *Codex Theodosianus cum Perpetuis Commentariis,* 6 vols., Leipzig, 1734.

Guilday, P., *History of the Councils of Baltimore,* New York, Macmillan, 1932.

Haring, J., *Das Neue Ehedekret Ne Temere,* Graz, Meyerhoff, 1907.

Hefele-Leclerque, *Histoire des Councils,* 5 vols., Paris, 1910.

Hilling, N., *Die Kanonische Form der Verlöbnisse und der Eheschliessung,* Bonn, Hanstein, 1915.

Hormann, W. Von, *Die Tridentinische Trauungsform,* Czernowitz, 1904.

Huebner, *History of Germanic Private Law* [vol. IV, of the Continental Legal History Series], translation of F. S. Philbrick, Boston, Little, Brown and Company, 1918.

Hyland, E., *Excommunication,* Washington, Catholic University, 1928.

Joyce, G. W., *Christian Marriage,* London and New York, Sheed and Ward, 1932.

Kearney, R., *Principles of Delegation,* Washington, Catholic University, 1929.

Knecht, A., *Die Neuen Eherechtlichen Dekrete,* Koln, Bachem, 1907.

——— *Handbuch des Katholischen Eherechts auf grund des Codex Iuris Canonici,* Freiburg in Breisgau, Herder, 1928.

Lehmkuhl, A., *Theologia Moralis,* 12 ed., 2 vols., Freiburg in Bresigau, Herder, 1914.

Leinz, A., *Die Ehevorschrift des Councils von Trient,* Freiburg in Breisgau, 1888.

Leitner, M., *Die Verlobungs-und Eheschliessungsform,* 6 ed., Regensburg, 1910.

——— *Lehrbuch des Katholischen Eherechts,* 3 ed., Paderborn, 1920.

LePlat, J., *Monumenta ad Historiam Concilii Tridentini,* 7 vols., Louvain, 1781.

Linneborn, J., *Grundriss des Eherechts,* 4 ed., Paderborn, 1933.

McNicholas, J., *The New Legislation on Engagements and Marriage,* Philadelphia, 1908.

Mansella, J., *De Impedimentis Matrimonium Dirimentibus ac de Processu Iudiciali in Causis Matrimonialibus Notiones et Disceptationes Canonicae,* Rome, 1881.

Maroto, P., *Institutiones Iuris Canonici,* 3 ed., 2 vols., Rome, apud Commentarium Pro Religiosis, 1921.

Meier, Ernst von, *Ius quod de Forma Matrimonii Valet, quomodo ex pristina iuris conditione profectum sit, disquiritur,* Berlin, ex typographia Gustavi Schade, 1856.

Müssener, H., *Das Katholische Eherecht,* Düsseldorf, L. Schwann, 1933.

Noldin, H., *Summa Theologiae Moralis iuxta Codicem Iuris Canonici,* 17 ed., revised by A. Schmitt, 3 vols., Innsbruck, Rausch, 1929.

Ojetti, B., *Commentarium in Codicem Iuris Canonici,* 3 vols., Rome, apud Aedes Universitatis Gregorianae, 1928.

Pallavicinus, Petrus, *Vera Concilii Tridentini Historia,* translated from the Italian by J. Baptista Giattino, S.J., 3 vols., Antverpiae, ex Officina Plantiniana, Baltasaria Noreti, 1670.

Pastor, Ludwig von, *History of the Popes from the Close of the Middle Ages,* 18 vols., London and St. Louis, 1891-1930.

Payen, G., *De Matrimonio in Missionibus ac Potissimum in Sinis Tractatus Practicus et Casus,* 3 vols., Zi-ka-wei, in Typographia T'OU-SE-WE, 1928-1929.

Perrone, J., *De Matrimonio Christiano,* 3 vols., Leodii, 1861.

Prümmer, Dominicus, *Manuale Theologiae Moralis,* 4 ed., 3 vols., Freiburg in Breisgau, Herder, 1928.

Roberts, *The Banns of Marriage,* Washington, Catholic University, 1931.

Rossi, J., *De Paroecia,* Rome, Pustet, 1923.

——— *De Matrimonii Celebratione iuxta Codicem Iuris Canonici,* Rome, Pustet, 1924.

Sanchez, Thomas, *Disputationum de Sancto Matrimonii Sacramento Libri Sex,* 3 vols., Geneva, 1602.

Schenk, F., *The Matrimonial Impediments of Mixed Religion and Disparity of Cult,* Washington, Catholic University, 1929.

Scherer, R., *Handbuch des Kirchenrechts,* 2 vols., Gran, 1898.
Schulte, J., *Lehrbuch des Katholischen Kirchenrechts,* Giessen, 1873.
Scott, S. P., *The Civil Law,* 7 vols., Central Trust Company, Cincinnati, 1932.
Sherman, C., *Roman Law in Modern World,* 2 ed., 3 vols., New York, Baker, Voorhis and Co., 1924.
Stockton, Louis, *Marriage from Legal and Ecclesiastical Viewpoint,* Buffalo, New York, Bleistern, 1912.
Trombetta, A., *Supplet Ecclesia, seu Commentarium in canon 209, C. I. C.,* Naples, M. d'Auria, 1931.
Van Hove, A., *De Legibus Ecclesiasticis,* Mechliniae-Romae, Dessain, 1930,
Vermeersch, A., *De Forma Sponsalium et Matrimonii post Decretum Ne Temere,* Bruges, 1908.
——— *Theologiae Moralis Principia, Responsa, Consilia,* 2 ed., 3 vols., Rome, Universitas Gregoriana, 1926-1928.
Vermeersch-Creusen, *Epitome Iuris Canonici,* 4 ed., 3 vols., Mechlinae, Dessain, 1929.
Vlaming, Thomas, *Praelectiones Iuris Canonici,* 3 ed., 2 vols., Bussum, 1919.
Vromant, G., *Ius Missionariorum,* vol. V; *De Matrimonio,* Louvain, Museum Lessianum, 1931.
Waterworth, J., *The Canons and Decrees of the Sacred and Oecumenical Council of Trent,* London, 1848.
Wernz, Franciscus, *Jus Decretalium,* vol IV in 2, Prati, ex Off. Lib. Giochetti, 1911-1913.
Wernz-Vidal, *Jus Canonicum,* vol. V, *Ius Matrimoniale,* 2 ed., Rome, apud Aedes Universitatis Gregorianae, 1928.
Westermarck, E., *The History of Human Marriage,* London, Macmillan, 1891.
Wouters, L., *De Forma Promissionis et Celebrationis Matrimonii,* 5 ed., Bussum, Brand, 1919.
Zitelli, Z., *Apparatus Iuris Ecclesiastici,* 3 ed., Ratisbonae, 1903.

Periodicals

American Ecclesiastical Review (AER), Philadelphia, 1889—
Apollinaris, Rome, 1928—
Archiv für katholisches Kirchenrecht (AKKR), Mainz, 1857—
Ephemerides Theologicae Lovanienses (ETL) Louvain, 1924—
Homiletic and Pastoral Review (HPR), New York, 1900—
Irish Ecclesiastical Record, The (IER), Dublin, 1864—
Ius Pontificium, Rome, 1921—
L'Ami du Clergé, Nancy, 1883—
Monitore Ecclesiastico (il), Rome, 1875—
Nouvelle Revue Theologique (NRT), Paris, 1869—
Periodica de re canonica et morali utili praesertim Religiosis et Missionariis, Bruges, 1905—
Theologisch-Praktische Quartalschrift (LQR), Linz, 1832—

UNIVERSITAS CATHOLICA AMERICAE

WASHINGTON, D. C.

FACULTAS JURIS CANONICI

No. 84

1934

ALPHABETICAL INDEX

BIOGRAPHICAL NOTE.

JOHN J. CARBERRY was born in Brooklyn, New York, July 31, 1904. After completing his elementary education at Saint Boniface Parochial School, Brooklyn, New York, he entered the diocesan Preparatory Seminary, Cathedral College of the Immaculate Conception, September, 1919. In November of 1924 he entered the seminary of the North American College in Rome, Italy, and was ordained to the priesthood, July 28, 1929. His philosophical and theological studies were made at the University of the Propaganda, Rome, Italy, where he received the degrees of Doctor in Philosophy and Doctor in Theology. In September, 1931, he entered the Catholic University to pursue a graduate course of studies in the School of Canon Law, where he received the Baccalaureate and Licentiate in Canon Law.

CANON LAW STUDIES

1. Freriks, Rev. Celestine A., C.PP.S., J.C.D., Religious Congregations in Their External Relations, 121 pp., 1916.
2. Galliher, Rev. Daniel M., O.P., J.C.D., Canonical Elections, 117 pp., 1917.
3. Borkowski, Rev. Aurelius L., O.F.M., De Confraternitatibus Ecclesiasticis, 136 pp., 1918.
4. Castillo, Rev. Cayo, J.C.D., Disertacion Historico-canonica sobre la Potestad del Cabildo en Sede Vacante o Impedida del Vicario Capitular, 99 pp., 1919 (1918).
5. Kubelbeck, Rev. William J., S.T.B., J.C.D., The Sacred Penitentiaria and Its Relations to Faculties of Ordinaries and Priests, 129 pp., 1918.
6. Petrovits, Rev. Joseph J. C., S.T.D., J.C.D., The New Church Law on Matrimony, X-461 pp., 1919.
7. Hickey, Rev. John J., S.T.B., J.C.D., Irregularities and Simple Impediments in the New Code of Canon Law, 100 pp., 1920.
8. Klekotka, Rev. Peter J., S.T.B., J.C.D., Diocesan Consultors, 179 pp., 1920.
9. Wannenmacher, Rev. Francis, J.C.D., The Evidence in Ecclesiastical Procedure Affecting the Marriage Bond, 1920. (Not Printed.)
10. Golden, Rev. Henry Francis, J.C.D., Parochial Benefices in the New Code, IV-119 pp., 1921. (Printed 1925.)
11. Koudelka, Rev. Charles, J., J.C.D., Pastors, Their Rights and Duties According to the New Code of Canon Law, 211 pp., 1921.
12. Melo, Rev. Antonius, O.F.M., J.C.D., De Exemptione Regularium, X-188 pp., 1921.
13. Schaaf, Rev. Valentine Theodore, O.F.M., S.T.B., J.C.D., The Cloister, X-180 pp., 1921.
14. Burke, Rev. Thomas Joseph, S.T.B., J.C.D., Competence in Ecclesiastical Tribunals, IV-117 pp., 1922.
15. Leech, Rev. George Leo, J.C.D., A Comparative Study of the Constitution "Apostolicae Sedis" and the "Codex Juris Canonici," 179 pp., 1922.
16. Motry, Rev. Hubert Louis, S.T.D., J.C.D., Diocesan Faculties According to the Code of Canon Law, II-167 pp., 1922.
17. Murphy, Rev. George Lawrence, J.C.D., Delinquencies and Penalties in the Administration and the Reception of the Sacraments, IV-121 pp., 1923.
18. O'Reilly, Rev. John Anthony, S.T.B., J.C.D., Ecclesiastical Sepulture in the New Code of Canon Law, II-129 pp., 1923.
19. Michalicka, Rev. Wenceslas Cyrill, O.S.B., J.C.D., Judicial Procedure in Dismissal of Clerical Exempt Religious, 107 pp., 1923.

20. Dargin, Rev. Edward Vincent, S.T.B., J.C.D., Reserved Cases According to the Code of Canon Law, IV-103 pp., 1924.

21. Godfrey, Rev. John A., S.T.B., J.C.D., The Right of Patronage According to the Code of Canon Law, 153 pp., 1924.

22 Hagedorn, Rev. Francis Edward, J.C.D., General Legislation on Indulgences, II-154 pp., 1924.

23. King, Rev. James Ignatius, J.C.D., The Administration of the Sacraments to Dying Non-Catholics, V-141 pp., 1924.

24. Winslow, Rev. Francis Joseph, A.F.M., J.C.D., Vicars and Prefects Apostolic, IV-149 pp., 1924.

25. Correa, Rev. Jose Servelion, S.T.L., J.C.D., La Potestad Legislativa de la Iglesia Católica, IV-127 pp., 1925.

26. Dugan, Rev. Henry Francis, M.A., J.C.D., The Judiciary Department of the Diocesan Curia, 87 pp., 1925.

27. Keller, Rev. Charles Frederick, S.T.B., J.C.D., Mass Stipends, 167 pp., 1925.

28. Paschang, Rev. John Linus, J.C.D., The Sacramentals According to the Code of Canon Law, 129 pp., 1925.

29. Piontek, Rev. Cyrillus, O.F.M., S.T.B., J.C.D., De Indulto Exclaustrationis necnon Saecularizationis, XIII-289 pp., 1925.

30. Kearney, Rev. Richard Joseph, S.T.B., J.C.D., Sponsors at Baptism According to the Code of Canon Law, IV-127 pp., 1925.

31. Bartlett, Rev. Chester Joseph, A.M., LL.B., J.C.D., The Tenure of Parochial Property in the United States of America, V-108 pp., 1926.

32. Kilker, Rev. Adrian Jerome, J.C.D., Extreme Unction, V-425 pp. 1926.

33. McCormick, Rev. Robert Emmett, J.C.D., Confessors of Religious, VIII-266 pp., 1926.

34. Miller, Rev. Newton Thomas, J.C.D., Founded Masses According to the Code of Canon Law, VII-93 pp., 1926.

35. Roelker, Rev. Edward G., S.T.D., J.C.D., Principles of Privilege According to the Code of Canon Law, XI-166 pp., 1926.

36. Bakalarczyk, Rev. Richardus, M.I.C., J.U.D., De Novitiatu, VIII-208 pp., 1927.

37. Pizzuti, Rev. Lawrence, O.F.M., J.U.L., De Parochis Religiosis, 1927. (Not Printed.)

38. Bliley, Rev. Nicholas Martin, O.S.B., J.C.D., Altars According to the Code of Canon Law, XIX-132 pp., 1927.

39. Brown, Brendan Francis, A.B., LL.M., J.U.D., The Canonical Juristic Personality with Special Reference to its Status in the United States of America, V-212 pp., 1927.

40. Cavanaugh, Rev. William Thomas, C.P., J.U.D., The Reservation of the Blessed Sacrament, VIII-101 pp., 1927.

41. Doheny, Rev. William J., C.S.C., A.B., J.U.D., Church Property: Modes of Acquisition, X-118 pp,. 1927

42. Feldhaus, Rev. Aloysius H., C.PP.S., J.C.D., Oratories, IX-141 pp., 1927.
43. Kelly, Rev. James Patrick, A.B., J.C.D., The Jurisdiction of the Simple Confessor, X-208 pp., 1927.
44. Neuberger, Rev. Nicholas J., J.C.D., Canon 6 or the Relation of the Codex Juris Canonici to the Preceding Legislation, V-95 pp., 1927.
45. O'Keeffe, Rev. Gerald Michael, J.C.D., Matrimonial Dispensations, Powers of Bishops, Priests, and Confessors, VIII-232 pp., 1927.
46. Quigley, Rev. Joseph, A.M., A.B., J.C.D., Condemned Societies, 139 pp., 1927.
47. Zaplotnik, Rev. Ioannes Leo, J.C.D., De Vicariis Foraneis, X-142 pp., 1927.
48. Duskie, Rev. John Aloysius, A.B., J.C.D., The Canonical Status of the Orientals in the United States, VIII-196 pp., 1928.
49. Hyland, Rev. Francis Edward, J.C.D., Excommunication, Its Nature, Historical Development and Effects, VIII-181 pp., 1928.
50. Reinmann, Rev. Gerald Joseph, O.M.C., J.C.D., The Third Order Secular of Saint Francis, 201 pp., 1928.
51. Schenk, Rev. Francis J., J.C.D., The Matrimonial Impediments of Mixed Religion and Disparity of Cult, XVI-318 pp., 1929.
52. Coady, Rev. John Joseph, S.T.D., J.U.D., A.M., The Appointment of Pastors, VIII-150 pp., 1929.
53. Kay, Rev. Thomas Henry, J.C.D., Competence in Matrimonial Procedure, VIII-164 pp., 1929.
54. Turner, Rev. Sidney Joseph, C.P., J.U.D., The Vow of Poverty, XLIX-217 pp., 1929.
55. Kearney, Rev. Raymond A., A.B., S.T.D., J.C.D., The Principles of Delegation, VII-149 pp., 1929.
56. Conran, Rev. Edward James, A.B., J.C.D., The Interdict, V-163 pp., 1930.
57. O'Neil, Rev. William H., J.C.D., Papal Rescripts of Favor, VII-218 pp., 1930.
58. Bastnagel, Rev. Clement Vincent, J.U.D., The Appointment of Parochial Adjutants and Assistants, XV-257 pp., 1930.
59. Ferry, Rev. William A., A.B., J.C.D., Stole Fees, X-107 pp., 1930.
60. Costello, Rev. John Michael, A.B., J.C.D., Domicile and Quasi-Domicile, VII-201 pp., 1930.
61. Kremer, Rev. Michael Nicholas, A.B., S.T.B., J.C.D., Church Support in the United States, VI-136 pp., 1930.
62. Angulo, Rev. Luis, C.M., J.C.D., Legislación de la Iglesia sobre la intención en la applicación de la Santa Misa, VII-104 pp., 1931.
63. Frey, Rev. Wolfgang Norbert, O.S.B., A.B., J.C.D., The Act of Religious Profession, VIII-174 pp., 1931.
64. Roberts, Rev. James Brendan, A.B., J.C.D., The Banns of Marriage, XIV-140 pp., 1931.

65. Ryder, Rev. Raymond Aloysius, A.B., J.C.D., Simony, IX-151 pp., 1931.
66. Campagna, Rev. Angelo, Ph.D., J.U.D., Il Vicario Generale del Vescovo, VII-205 pp., 1931.
67. Cox, Rev. Joseph Godfrey, A.B., J.C.D., The Administration of Seminaries, VI-124 pp., 1931.
68. Gregory, Rev. Donald J., J.U.D., The Pauline Privilege, XV-165 pp., 1931.
60. Donohue, Rev. John F., J.C.D., The Impediment of Crime, VIII-110 pp., 1931.
70. Dooley, Rev. Eugene A., O.M.I., J.C.D., Church Law on Sacred Relics, IX-143 pp., 1931.
71. Orth, Rev. Clement Raymond, O.M.C., J.C.D., The Approbation of Religious Institutes, 171 pp., 1931.
72. Pernicone, Rev. Joseph M., A.B., J.C.D., The Ecclesiastical Prohibition of Books, XII-267 pp., 1932.
73. Clinton, Rev. Connell, A.B., J.C.D., The Paschal Precept, IX-108 pp., 1932.
74. Donnelly, Rev. Francis B., A.M., S.T.L., J.C.D., The Diocesan Synod, VIII-125 pp., 1932
75. Torrente, Rev. Camilo, C.M.F., J.C.D., Las Processiones Sagradas, V-145 pp., 1932.
76. Murphy, Rev. Edwin J., C.PP.S., J.C.D., Suspension Ex Informata Conscientia, XI-122 pp., 1932.
77. MacKenzie, Rev. Eric F., A.M., S.T.L., J.C.D., The Delict of Heresy in its Commission, Penalization, Absolution, VII-124 pp., 1932.
78. Lyons, Rev. Avitus E., S.T.B., J.C.D., The Collegiate Tribunal of First Instance, XI-147 pp., 1932.
79. Connolly, Rev. Thomas A., J.C.D., Appeals, XI-195 pp., 1932.
80. Sangmeister, Rev. Joseph V., A.B., J.C.D., Force and Fear as Precluding Matrimonial Consent, V-211 pp., 1932.
81. Jaeger, Rev. Leo A., A.B., J.C.D., The Administration of Vacant and Quasi-Vacant Episcopal Sees in the United States, IX-229 pp. 1932.
82. Rimlinger, Rev. Herbert T., J.C.D., Error Invalidating Matrimonial Consent, VII-79 pp., 1932.
83. Barrett, Rev. John D. M., S.S., J.C.D., Comparative Study of the Third Plenary Council and the Code, IX-221 pp., 1932.
84. Carberry, Rev. John J., Ph.D., S.T.D., J.C.L., The Juridical Form of Marriage, 1934.
85. Dolan, Rev. John L., A.B., J.C.L., The Defensor Vinculi, 1934.
86. Hannan, Rev. Jerome D., A.M., S.T.D., LL.B., J.C.L., The Cannon Law of Wills, 1934.
87. Lemieux, Rev. Lelisle A., A.M., J.C.L., The Sentence in Ecclesiastical Procedure, 1934.
88. O'Rourke, Rev. James J., A.B., J.C.L., Parish Registers, 1934.

89. TIMLIN, REV. BARTHOLOMEW, O.F.M., A.M., J.C.L., Conditional Matrimonial Consent, 1934.
90. WAHL, REV. FRANCIS X., A.B., J.C.L., The Matrimonial Impediments of Consanguinity and Affinity, 1934.
91. WHITE, REV. ROBERT J., A.B., LL.B., S.T.B., J.C.L., Canonical Ante-Nuptial Promises and the Civil Law, 1934.

www.ingramcontent.com/pod-product-compliance
Lightning Source LLC
LaVergne TN
LVHW050233080826
844660LV00012B/526

* 9 7 8 0 8 1 3 2 2 2 7 3 8 *